DNA Evidence and Investigation

Peggy J. Parks

Current Issues

ReferencePoint
Press®

San Diego, CA

© 2010 ReferencePoint Press, Inc.

For more information, contact:
ReferencePoint Press, Inc.
PO Box 27779
San Diego, CA 92198
www.ReferencePointPress.com

Picture credits:
Cover: Dreamstime and iStockphoto.com
AP Images: 11, 14
Steve Zmina: 30–32, 44–46, 60–62, 75–77

LIBRARY OF CONGRESS CATALOGING-IN-PUBLICATION DATA

Parks, Peggy J., 1951–
  DNA evidence and investigation / by Peggy J. Parks.
    p. cm. -- (Compact research series)
  Includes bibliographical references.
  ISBN-13: 978-1-60152-102-6 (hardback)
  ISBN-10: 1-60152-102-2 (hardback)
 1. Criminal investigation—Juvenile literature. 2. Forensic sciences—Juvenile literature.
 3. DNA fingerprinting—Juvenile literature. I. Title.
  HV8073.8.P44 2009
  363.25'62—dc22
                                                        2009033236

Contents

Foreword

As modern civilization continues to evolve, its ability to create, store, distribute, and access information expands exponentially. The explosion of information from all media continues to increase at a phenomenal rate. By 2020 some experts predict the worldwide information base will double every 73 days. While access to diverse sources of information and perspectives is paramount to any democratic society, information alone cannot help people gain knowledge and understanding. Information must be organized and presented clearly and succinctly in order to be understood. The challenge in the digital age becomes not the creation of information, but how best to sort, organize, enhance, and present information.

ReferencePoint Press developed the *Compact Research* series with this challenge of the information age in mind. More than any other subject area today, researching current issues can yield vast, diverse, and unqualified information that can be intimidating and overwhelming for even the most advanced and motivated researcher. The *Compact Research* series offers a compact, relevant, intelligent, and conveniently organized collection of information covering a variety of current topics ranging from illegal immigration and deforestation to diseases such as anorexia and meningitis.

The series focuses on three types of information: objective single-author narratives, opinion-based primary source quotations, and facts and statistics. The clearly written objective narratives provide context and reliable background information. Primary source quotes are carefully selected and cited, exposing the reader to differing points of view. And facts and statistics sections aid the reader in evaluating perspectives. Presenting these key types of information creates a richer, more balanced learning experience.

For better understanding and convenience, the series enhances information by organizing it into narrower topics and adding design features that make it easy for a reader to identify desired content. For example, in *Compact Research: Illegal Immigration*, a chapter covering the economic impact of illegal immigration has an objective narrative explaining the various ways the economy is impacted, a balanced section of numerous primary source quotes on the topic, followed by facts and full-color illustrations to encourage evaluation of contrasting perspectives.

The ancient Roman philosopher Lucius Annaeus Seneca wrote, "It is quality rather than quantity that matters." More than just a collection of content, the *Compact Research* series is simply committed to creating, finding, organizing, and presenting the most relevant and appropriate amount of information on a current topic in a user-friendly style that invites, intrigues, and fosters understanding.

DNA Evidence and Investigation at a Glance

DNA Defined

Deoxyribonucleic acid (DNA) is a molecule that carries the biological instructions for all living things. Within the nuclei of the body's cells, DNA is tightly bundled inside chromosomes, and it is also found in structures inside cells known as mitochondria.

How DNA Evidence Is Used

DNA evidence is used to solve a wide variety of crimes but it is most often used in rape and murder cases.

DNA Collection

DNA may be found in skin cells, fingernails, saliva, bones, blood, semen, and teeth, among other sources. Objects such as drinking glasses or cups, cigarette butts, articles of clothing, and used condoms may contain DNA that could connect a suspect to a crime scene.

DNA Analysis

Forensic scientists extract DNA from samples and then scan 13 different regions known as loci, which involves scrutinizing two genetic markers on each of the loci. If a match is found on all 13 loci, the DNA is virtually certain to be that of the suspect.

Crime Database

The Combined DNA Index System (CODIS) is a central database maintained by the FBI that contains DNA profiles from crime laboratories throughout the United States.

Conclusiveness of DNA Evidence

Although no evidence is 100 percent accurate, many forensic scientists say that DNA is superior to all other types of evidence, especially eyewitness testimony.

Forensic Lab Errors

A 2009 report by the National Research Council revealed that crime laboratories throughout the United States use forensic techniques that are badly flawed. The study noted that DNA technology is the only forensic technique that has been scientifically proven to connect crime scene evidence to a suspect.

Exonerating the Wrongfully Accused

DNA is as effective at clearing people who have been wrongfully accused as it is at solving crimes. As of August 2009, 242 prisoners in the United States had been exonerated due to DNA evidence; 17 of those were on death row.

The Right to DNA Testing

Although the U.S. Supreme Court has ruled that the Constitution does not ensure DNA testing for prisoners, 47 states have legislation in place that allows for such testing under certain circumstances.

DNA Databases and Civil Liberties

Once someone's DNA is in the CODIS database, his or her complete genetic information may be on file. Because police, forensic scientists, and certain others can access the DNA without the person's consent, many view this as an invasion of privacy and a threat to civil liberties.

Overview

❝In case after case, DNA has proven what scientists already know—that eyewitness identification is frequently inaccurate.❞

—Innocence Project, a national litigation and public policy organization dedicated to exonerating wrongfully convicted people through DNA testing.

❝DNA identification can be quite effective if used intelligently.❞

—The Human Genome Project, a genetic research agency of the U.S. Department of Energy's Office of Science.

On June 3, 2009, a federal jury in Greenbelt, Maryland, convicted Earl Whittley Davis of armed robbery, carjacking, and murder. Five years before, Davis had shot and killed Jason Schwindler, an employee of an armored car company who was walking into a bank to deliver more than $50,000 in cash. After Davis and an accomplice shot Schwindler multiple times, they grabbed the bag of money and climbed into a Jeep that was parked in front of the bank. To prevent their escape the armored car driver slammed into the Jeep, rendering it inoperable. The 2 men ran to the back of the bank and, at gunpoint, demanded that a customer give them her keys. They fled the scene in her car.

Two months later police tracked Davis down and arrested him. They found him by analyzing DNA samples on the steering wheel of the Jeep and the stolen car, as well as on a baseball cap that he had left behind. "Earl Davis will never again be able to commit a murder on the streets of Prince George's County," says U.S. attorney Rod J. Rosenstein. "A jury verdict cannot replace a lost life, but it brings a small measure of justice for Jason Schwindler, a 28-year-old Navy veteran and a husband and father, who was brutally murdered during an armored car robbery."[1]

The Blueprint of Life

Inside the human body are trillions of cells that perform various functions, from fighting infection to carrying oxygen throughout the blood vessels. The cells that have a nucleus (such as white blood cells) contain deoxyribonucleic acid, or DNA, a molecule that carries the biological instructions for all living things to develop and survive. Within the cells' nuclei, DNA is tightly bundled inside long, threadlike structures called chromosomes. The National Human Genome Research Institute explains: "DNA spends a lot of time in its chromosome form. But during cell division, DNA unwinds so it can be copied and the copies transferred to new cells. DNA also unwinds so that its instructions can be used to make proteins and for other biological processes."[2] In addition to DNA that originates in the nuclei of cells (known as nuclear DNA), DNA is also found inside mitochondria, which are structures inside cells that convert food energy into nourishment for cells. This is known as mitochondrial DNA. Together all the DNA that makes up a person's body is known as the genome.

With the exception of identical twins, the DNA of every human being is unique to him or her, and it does not change throughout someone's life. As a result, in those who are not identical twins, it is virtually impossible for two people to have the exact same DNA. In a 2008 report by the Urban Institute, the authors write: "The likelihood that any two nonidentical siblings have the same . . . DNA profile can be as little as one in one billion or more."[3] Because DNA is so individualized, it is often considered the most valuable and reliable type of evidence in solving crimes.

How DNA Evidence Is Used

DNA evidence is most frequently used to identify people who have committed violent crimes or to *exclude* people as suspects. Because DNA evidence is not always available and because, when it is available, collection and analysis is expensive, it is used less often in property crimes. According to the U.S. Department of Justice, however, that is starting to change. Costs are falling and awareness of the value of DNA evidence as a tool for solving numerous types of crime is growing.

How DNA Evidence Is Collected and Analyzed

DNA can be extracted from innumerable sources, including hair, fingernails, saliva, bones, blood, semen, teeth, and even dandruff and ear wax. It may be collected from objects such as hats, eyeglasses, coffee cups, cigarette butts, bottles and cans, and used condoms, any of which could connect a suspect to a crime. After a crime has been committed, evidence is collected from the scene. In the case of a rape, for example, the victim's body becomes the "crime scene" and is thoroughly examined, usually by a physician or someone who specializes in sexual assaults. As an April 2009 *New York Times* article explains, the victim is "typically asked to undress over a large sheet of white paper to collect hairs or fibers, and then her body is examined with an ultraviolet light, photographed and thoroughly swabbed for the rapist's DNA. It's a grueling and invasive process that can last four to six hours and produces a 'rape kit.'"[4]

> As awareness of the value of DNA evidence continues to grow, its use is becoming more widespread in solving numerous types of crime.

Once a suspect has been identified, a DNA sample is taken from the person, and forensic scientists scan 13 different regions known as loci. This involves scrutinizing 2 genetic markers (1 that has been inherited from each parent), on each of the loci. If a match is found on all 13 loci, the DNA is virtually certain to be that of the suspect. The Human Genome Project explains:

"With DNA . . . you can look for matches (based on sequence or on numbers of small repeating units of DNA sequence) at many different locations on the person's genome; one or two (even three) aren't enough to be confident that the suspect is the right one, but thirteen sites are used. A match at all thirteen is rare enough that you (or a prosecutor or a jury) can be very confident ('beyond a reasonable doubt') that the right person is accused."[5]

Once the analysis is complete, forensic scientists use the data to create a DNA profile of that individual, which is sometimes called a DNA

A forensic specialist gathers evidence on a blood-covered sidewalk where a shooting took place. The DNA found in blood, skin cells, saliva, and other bodily fluids can connect a suspect to a crime, making DNA testing a valuable law enforcement tool.

fingerprint. The scientists also use the same basic technique to extract DNA from evidence that was taken from the crime scene and use the DNA to create a forensic profile.

America's DNA Database

If a crime has been committed and no suspects have been identified, a forensic DNA profile from crime scene evidence can be entered into the FBI's Combined DNA Index System (CODIS). This is a central database that contains DNA profiles from laboratories throughout the United States. CODIS is a 3-tiered system with separate local, state, and national databases. The FBI explains: "That way, local and state labs can maintain DNA databases according to their own laws and needs, but still search for matches at the national level."[6] The national tier is called the National DNA Index System, or NDIS, and it is maintained by the FBI. CODIS uses 2 indexes to gather investigative leads in which DNA evidence has been collected. One, known as the Convicted Offender Index, contains profiles of everyone who has been convicted of violent crimes. The other is the Forensic Index, which contains DNA profiles that have been developed from evidence collected at crime scenes. According to the FBI, as of June 2009 the database contained more than 7 million offender profiles and 272,000 forensic profiles and had assisted in tens of thousands of criminal investigations.

> "If a crime has been committed and no suspects have been identified, a forensic DNA profile from crime scene evidence can be entered into the FBI's Combined DNA Index System (CODIS)."

The Justice Department says that the amount of data in state and national DNA databases is growing, and many DNA databases now include DNA profiles of all convicted felons, whether they committed violent or nonviolent crimes. This is because researchers have found that many offenders convicted of nonviolent crimes do not limit their activities to property-related crimes and often commit other offenses as well, including violent crimes and drug deals. "For example," the Justice Department writes, "a Florida study revealed that 52 percent of that state's DNA database 'hits' against murder and sexual assault cases matched individuals who were originally placed in the database for burglary convictions. A hit occurs when a database search of a DNA profile from biological evidence matches a profile in the database, thus identifying a suspect."[7]

How Conclusive Is DNA Evidence in Solving Crimes?

With any crime, no evidence can be said to be 100 percent accurate, including DNA. For instance, if a person had visited the scene before the crime was committed, his or her DNA could be inaccurately implicated. In some cases DNA may be contaminated, either due to careless collection at a crime scene or errors made at a forensic laboratory. And there is always the chance, although extremely slight, that unrelated people could share the same DNA profile.

Nevertheless, DNA is considered to be a highly effective way of identifying suspects, and many forensic scientists say that it is superior to all other types of evidence. This is particularly true with eyewitness testimony, which has proved to be inaccurate at least half of the time when used to identify someone accused of a crime. This is often because of mistaken identity, such as witnesses incorrectly identifying suspects from police lineups or mug shots, but eyewitnesses may also deliberately lie about people whom they implicate in crimes. More accurate than eyewitness testimony are fingerprints, but even they are not always reliable, especially if only a partial or smudged print has been found.

How Effective Is DNA Testing for Correcting Justice System Errors?

According to the Innocence Project, an organization dedicated to exonerating wrongfully convicted people through DNA testing, 242 prisoners had been exonerated due to DNA evidence in the United States as of September 2009. One of the most recent was Chaunte Ott, a man originally from Milwaukee, Wisconsin. Ott was arrested in 1995 on suspicion of raping 16-year-old Jessica Payne and brutally stabbing her to death. At trial the following year, Ott pleaded not guilty but was convicted of murder and sentenced to life in prison. Several years later, with the help of the Wisconsin Innocence Project, DNA testing found evidence that another man—not Ott—had actually been involved in the rape and murder. Ott was released from prison in January 2009. "It was like . . . I can't even express the gratitude I felt for the lawyers who believed in me and seen the facts for what they were," he told reporters. "It's a dream come true. It's the greatest feeling in the world."[8]

> According to the Innocence Project, an organization dedicated to exonerating wrongfully convicted people through DNA testing, 242 prisoners had been exonerated due to DNA evidence in the United States as of September 2009.

Should Prisoners Have a Right to DNA Testing?

In June 2009 the Supreme Court made a controversial ruling about DNA tests for convicted criminals—the tests are not guaranteed under the U.S. Constitution. The majority of justices ruled that the decision of

A forensic scientist extracts DNA from crime scene samples. Although dozens of convicted offenders have been exonerated of crimes because of DNA evidence and testing, such tests are not a constitutional right, the U.S. Supreme Court ruled in 2009.

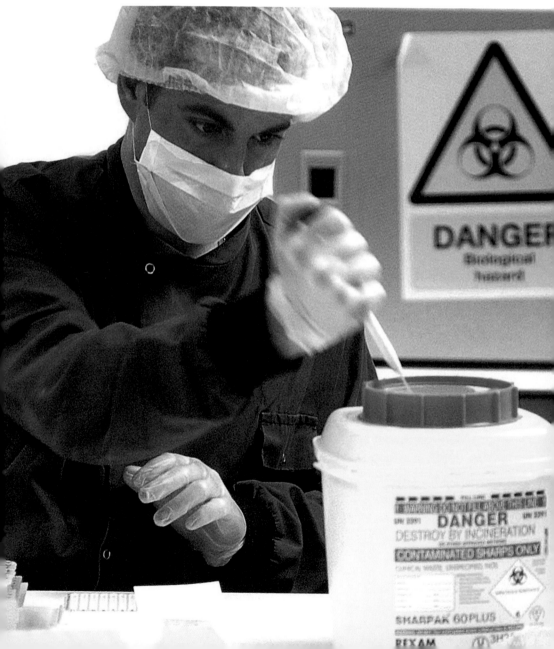

whether to permit DNA testing should be left up to the individual states. The justices wrote:

> To suddenly constitutionalize this area would short-circuit what has been a prompt and considered legislative response by Congress and the States. It would shift to the Federal Judiciary responsibility for devising rules governing DNA access and creating a new constitutional code of procedures to answer the myriad questions that would arise. There is no reason to suppose that federal courts' answers to those questions will be any better than those of state courts and legislatures, and good reason to suspect the opposite.[9]

Even in the absence of a constitutional guarantee for postconviction DNA testing, 47 states have legislation in place that make such tests possible. But according to the Innocence Project, many of these laws are limited in scope and substance. Studies have shown that prosecutors throughout the country often oppose DNA testing for convicted criminals. As a May 2009 article in the *New York Times* states: "Prosecutors say they are concerned that convicts will seek DNA testing as a delay tactic or a fishing expedition, and that allowing DNA tests undermines hard-won jury verdicts and opens the floodgates to overwhelming requests."[10]

> " In June 2009 the Supreme Court made a controversial ruling about DNA tests for convicted criminals—the tests are not guaranteed under the U.S. Constitution. "

Do Law Enforcement DNA Databases Threaten Civil Liberties?

As effective a tool as DNA technology has proved to be, it involves some touchy legal, ethical, and social issues. For instance, once someone's DNA is in the CODIS database, his or her complete genetic information, including family relationships and susceptibility to disease, may be on file. Police, forensic scientists, and certain others can access the DNA without the person's consent, which is viewed by many as an invasion of privacy. Also, a growing number of states have laws in place that allow DNA evidence to be collected when someone has been arrested or detained for a crime but has not been found guilty. Those who oppose such practices say that this is a violation of civil rights because the DNA of innocent people will likely be on file along with those who have been convicted of crimes.

Another objection to DNA databases is that many state laws do not require the destruction of DNA samples and/or records after a conviction has been overturned by the courts. Thus, the DNA of those who have not committed crimes remains in the national database. However, in Florida, one of the states that allows DNA to be collected after a felony arrest, rather than only after a conviction, the law calls for such evidence to be purged from the state's DNA database. Gerald Bailey, commissioner of the Florida Department of Law Enforcement, explains:

> "Florida's carefully crafted legislation contains key protections. There are clear provisions for removal of DNA from the database if a person arrested for a felony is acquitted, the case is overturned, dismissed or not prosecuted."[11]

Traditionally, the FBI only retained DNA on file for criminals convicted of federal crimes. But in April 2009 the agency announced that it had vastly expanded its database. It will now also include DNA samples from those who have been *arrested* for crimes and are awaiting trial, as well as non-U.S. citizens who are being detained in the United States. Senator Patrick Leahy, who is chair of the Senate Judiciary Committee, adamantly opposed the expansion of the FBI's database, as he explains: "This change adds little or no value for law enforcement, while intruding on the privacy rights of people who are, in our system, presumed innocent. It creates an incentive for [arbitrary] arrests, and will likely have a disproportionate impact on minorities and the poor. This policy may also make it harder for innocent people to have their DNA expunged from government databases."[12]

> " As effective a tool as DNA technology has proved to be, it involves some touchy legal, ethical, and social issues. "

Using Familial DNA to Catch Criminals

A particularly controversial issue is whether DNA from family members of a suspect should be used to track down criminals. Many law enforcement officials support what is known as familial DNA testing. If a suspect's DNA is not available, a member of his or her immediate family will likely be a very close match because DNA is inherited.

One of the most famous cases of a criminal caught by familial DNA testing was the arrest of Dennis Rader in 2005. Years before, Rader had committed a string of brutal murders in the Wichita, Kansas, area, during which he tortured his victims before killing them and then left letters at the crime scenes signed "BTK" for "bind, torture, kill." Rader eluded law enforcement for nearly 3 decades, beginning in 1974 when he committed the first murders until 2004 when he reemerged after 14 years of silence. When he sent e-mail messages warning authorities that he was about to strike again, forensic investigators tracked him down through the computer that he had used to send the e-mails. They lacked evidence that would tie Rader to the crimes, so prosecutors obtained a court order to examine the DNA of his daughter Kerri by analyzing her routine Pap smear. The DNA was compared to evidence taken from several murder scenes, and it was nearly a perfect match, indicating that Rader was almost certainly guilty of the crimes. Investigators then used the evidence to arrest Rader, who confessed that he was indeed the BTK murderer. He was convicted of committing multiple murders and was sentenced to 10 consecutive life terms in prison.

> " A particularly controversial issue is whether DNA from family members of a suspect should be used to track down criminals. "

Many prosecutors and other law enforcement professionals say that familial DNA is a powerful tool that could vastly increase the number of suspects who are caught and punished for committing crimes. Others disagree, arguing that the practice turns family members into DNA informants, often without their knowledge or consent. American Civil

Liberties Union science advisor Tania Simoncelli strongly objects to using familial DNA to identify criminals, as she explains: "If practiced routinely, we would be subjecting hundreds of thousands of innocent people who happen to be relatives of individuals in the FBI database to lifelong genetic surveillance."[13]

Crime Lab Deficiencies

In September 2009 the National Research Council released the results of a two-year study that focused on examining forensic techniques used to solve crimes in laboratories throughout the country. The comprehensive report, which is entitled *Strengthening Forensic Science in the United States: A Path Forward,* revealed serious flaws in many long-established forensic techniques such as eyewitness testimony and fingerprints. The study found that there were no national standards for the processing of forensic evidence, no standardized procedures for many forensic science disciplines, and no uniformity in the certification of forensic practitioners. It also revealed that one out of every five crime labs in the United States does not meet accreditation standards set by the National Academy of Crime Lab Directors.

DNA Testing in the Future

Despite its controversial aspects, DNA is believed to hold great promise for crime investigation. Scientists continue to explore ways to increase DNA's ability to help law enforcement catch criminals and exonerate those who have been accused or convicted of crimes they did not commit. One of the challenges that still exists is that DNA analysis is expensive, although the cost has begun to decrease and use of DNA evidence is becoming more widespread. Scientists are aggressively exploring ways to perfect DNA technology and put it to use in solving a wider variety of crimes. As this research continues, DNA evidence will undoubtedly become even more important than it is today.

How Conclusive Is DNA Evidence in Solving Crimes?

> ❝In the past 20 years, DNA testing has radically transformed the field of forensic science. DNA's ability to accurately and precisely identify the guilty and exonerate the innocent has quickly set a new standard for forensic evidence.❞
>
> —John Grisham, a former criminal law attorney who is now an author of suspense fiction and a member of the Innocence Project's board of directors.

> ❝Physical evidence will always be important. Unfortunately, there is no DNA to be found at the scenes of many serious crimes.❞
>
> —Robert Bazell, chief science and health correspondent for MSNBC.

Today DNA evidence is used to catch and convict criminals who have committed a wide variety of crimes. It can be used to solve property crimes such as robbery and burglary, but it is most commonly used in sexual assault and murder cases. This is due to 2 factors: the added cost for DNA testing and analysis, and the higher likelihood that biological evidence can be recovered after a rape or murder. One serial rapist who was caught because of DNA evidence is Thomas James Parker, a business owner from Tierrasanta, California. In July 2009 Parker snuck into a woman's garage, grabbed her from behind in a bear hug, and held a knife against her throat, warning her not to make any noise. At first she did as he said, but then she fought back, kicking and screaming, and he fled the scene. He was captured a few blocks away and taken to jail. Because aspects of the crime were similar to those of 7 rapes that had previously been committed in the area, police suspected Parker was the rapist in those other cases. This was confirmed when testing showed that his DNA matched the DNA of semen that was found on 3 of the 7 victims. Officers planned to charge Parker with all 7 sexual assaults—but before he could be arraigned, he committed suicide by hanging himself in his jail cell.

Relatively New Technology

Scientists have been aware of DNA and its structure since the 1950s, but the advent of DNA testing occurred much more recently. In 1985 English geneticist Alec Jeffreys discovered that certain regions of DNA contain sequences that are repeated over and over again, and the number of repeated sections differs from person to person. This finding allowed him to develop a technique to perform human identity tests using DNA samples; thus, the first DNA test was born.

> Scientists have been aware of DNA and its structure since the 1950s, but the advent of DNA testing occurred much more recently.

In 1987 Jeffreys was approached by police officers from Leicestershire, England. They wanted his help in solving 2 separate cases, both of which involved the rape and murder of 15-year-old girls whose attacker was never found. Using Jeffreys's technique, the officers had thousands of males who lived or worked in the town undergo DNA tests, but none of the samples matched the semen taken from the victims. Later the police were informed of a conversation that was overheard in which a man said that he had taken the test in place of his friend, Colin Pitchfork. Police arrested Pitchfork, tested him, and found that his DNA perfectly matched the DNA in the semen samples taken from the girls. In 1987 Pitchfork became the first person ever to be convicted using DNA evidence, and the following year he was sentenced to life in prison.

Comparing DNA to Other Evidence

No evidence, DNA included, can ever be considered 100 percent accurate. But many law enforcement officials and forensic scientists say that DNA is as close to infallible as any evidence could possibly be. University of Chicago economics professor Steven D. Levitt explains its superiority over other evidence: "The bottom line is that DNA testing is not perfect, but it is still a million (or maybe a thousand?) times better than anything else we have to catch criminals."[14]

How DNA compares to other forensic evidence was the subject of a study that was done by the Urban Institute and published in March 2008. The study, known as the DNA Field Experiment, examined the effectiveness of DNA evidence in high-volume crimes such as burglary and vehicle theft. Between November 2005 and July 2007, researchers in California, Colorado, Arizona, and Kansas collected biological evidence from 500 crime scenes in each of 5 cities. The researchers found that DNA was at least 5 times more likely to result in suspect identification than fingerprints. They also found that in property crime cases where DNA evidence was processed, more than twice as many suspects were identified and arrested, and more than twice as many cases were accepted for prosecution. Additionally, they discovered that suspects who

> A particularly crucial discovery was that suspects who were identified by DNA had at least *twice as many* prior felony arrests and convictions as those identified by traditional investigation.

were identified by DNA had at least *twice as many* prior felony arrests and convictions as those identified by traditional investigation.

Also included in the written report was a synopsis of the United Kingdom's use of DNA evidence in catching and convicting criminals. In 2000 the British Home Office increased funding so that law enforcement officials in England and Wales would be able to collect DNA at a much larger number of crime scenes, including property crimes. In the years since the program was expanded, there has been a substantial improvement in the identification of crime suspects. For instance, the overall detection rate for burglaries when DNA evidence is used is 41 percent, compared with just 16 percent when other evidence is used. An estimated 50 percent of the cases that involved identifying criminals through DNA led to conviction, and 25 percent of those led to a prison sentence. The report also stated that police officers in the United Kingdom place a higher value on DNA identification over fingerprints when considering the most important forensic evidence in suspect identification.

DNA and Arson

Although only a small percentage of arson cases are ever solved (5 to 7 percent according to the FBI), DNA evidence can sometimes be recovered at the scene of a fire. Robert Rowe, who is a certified fire investigator and the owner of the consulting firm Pyrocop, explains: "DNA. What a wonderful thing. Whether it's a discarded cigarette, a drop of sweat or a strand of hair in a baseball cap or glove, DNA is one of the best forms of evidence available to the fire investigator. If you're an arsonist, you should probably invest in a fully encapsulated suit, which may be somewhat conspicuous if you're trying to be covert about your crime."[15]

> " Although only a small percentage of arson cases are ever solved (5 to 7 percent according to the FBI), DNA evidence can sometimes be recovered at the scene of a fire. "

In January 2009 a man from Baltimore was arrested for intentionally setting his nephew's two cars and home on fire the previous year. Charles Earnest Maynard had left a bottle behind that he used to make a Molotov cocktail, but the device did not explode. Investigators recovered the bottle and found traces of Maynard's DNA inside it, which led to his arrest. It was the first time county law enforcement had ever used DNA evidence to investigate arson. "This is a huge case for us," says police chief Matthew Tobia. "It signals that we're really raising the bar. Frequently, fire destroys a lot of the evidence, but in [this] case, we were able to collect DNA from the scene and use advanced techniques to match it (to Maynard)."[16]

Solving Cold Cases

DNA technology is now often used to solve cold cases, which are crimes that police have been unable to solve. In many cases these are crimes that were committed before the development of DNA technology or while the technology was in its infancy. According to the National Institute of Justice, more than 30 cold cases have been solved with DNA profiles contained in the CODIS database. Through the agency's Solving Cold Cases with DNA grant program, state and local governments receive funds that help them identify, review, investigate, and analyze homicide and rape cold cases that have the potential to be solved through DNA analysis. Since the program started in July 2004, it has received more than 200 requests for funding from law enforcement agencies around the country.

In one such case DNA evidence led to a woman who had murdered her baby—and she remained at large for 18 years. On November 12, 1991, a witness said that he was by a lake near Warner, Oklahoma, when he heard a woman scream. He was quite a distance away, but he could see that she was on the ground and a man was reaching between her legs. At that point he realized that the woman had just given birth, and he watched the man put the baby in a plastic bag and throw it on the ground. The couple left the area, and the witness rushed over to help, but he found that the infant was already dead. He called the police, who spent years chasing down dozens of leads, to no avail.

The case was finally closed but was reopened in 2003 in the hope that improved DNA technology could reveal the identity of the baby's parents. DNA samples taken from the scene at the time the crime was committed as well as from the infant were entered into CODIS. In 2008 this led to identification of the father. But because he was nowhere near the area where the crime took place and is a different race from the man the witness saw, police did not consider him a suspect. Then in 2009 the database was searched again, and a match came back for a 37-year-old woman named Penny Lowry, who at the time was residing in Virginia. Her DNA matched samples found at the crime scene, and she was arrested and charged with first-degree murder. As of July 2009 police were still hunting for her accomplice.

> **According to the National Institute of Justice, more than 30 cold cases have been solved with DNA profiles contained in the CODIS database.**

Human and Lab Errors

As reliable and accurate as DNA evidence has proved to be, improper evidence gathering and/or processing can result in serious errors. Investigations have shown that many convictions have resulted from testing errors at crime laboratories in a number of major cities. Tim O'Toole, an attorney from Washington, D.C., says that many who work in criminal justice have the mistaken belief that forensic crime labs are infallible. "It's a complete myth," he says. "This is a nationwide problem that has risen up in jurisdictions around the country. State and local crime labs have been rife with error and they've made a substantial number of mistakes."[17] For instance, a 2007 investigation of a crime lab in Massachusetts revealed that evidence from 16,000 crime scenes was never analyzed.

> "In addition to the risk of human error, another possible limitation of DNA evidence is the chance, although extremely slim, that it could identify the wrong suspect."

Houston, Texas, has also had serious crime lab problems. From 2002 to 2006, and again in 2007, the city's DNA lab was shut down after an audit uncovered numerous errors. A total of 160 convictions were identified as having flawed blood sample evidence, and lawyers were investigating whether that had possibly led to people being convicted for crimes that they did not commit. The first prisoner to be exonerated after the Houston crime lab scandal became public was Josiah Sutton, who had been sentenced to 25 years in prison for rape. New DNA testing showed that the crime lab had erred and that his DNA did not match what was found on the victim. "People might think [forensic science is] infallible," says O'Toole. "But science is only as good as the humans who perform it."[18]

In addition to the risk of human error, another possible limitation of DNA evidence is the chance, although extremely slim, that it could identify the wrong suspect. This was brought to light in 2008, when Arizona crime lab analyst Kathryn Troyer ran tests on the state's DNA evidence. During her analysis Troyer found 122 DNA profiles that were remarkably similar, with one pair matching 9 of 13 loci. According to the FBI, the odds of 2 unrelated people sharing those genetic markers are about 1 in 113 billion. Yet the 2 men who made up that pair were not related. After her discovery, Troyer found other people who also had close genetic markers. She says that this underscores how crucial it is for forensic scientists to analyze 13 loci rather than only 9, which was a common practice in the past and could lead investigators to implicate the wrong person. As Troyer's colleague Todd Griffith explains: "If you're going to search at nine loci, you need to be aware of what it means. It's not necessarily absolutely the guy."[19]

Addressing Flaws in Forensic Science

With the release of its September 2009 report *Strengthening Forensic Science in the United States: A Path Forward,* the National Research Council is hopeful that crime laboratories will begin taking steps to correct errors. The authors of the report made specific recommendations for how these flaws can be corrected, including the creation of a national agency that would oversee forensic science. Other suggestions included the development of routine, mandatory proficiency testing for people who work with forensic evidence, mandatory certification of forensic science professionals, and mandatory accreditation for crime laboratories. In order to make the necessary changes, the Council urges the U.S. Congress to allocate more funding for forensic science. This would set a national standard, and allow the National Institute of Forensic Science to work with other government agencies to prepare forensic scientists and crime scene investigators for their roles in managing and analyzing evidence.

Looking Ahead

Since 1985, when Alec Jeffreys developed the first DNA test, DNA technology has continued to grow more sophisticated and is now used to solve numerous crimes, from rape and murder to arson. Although not foolproof, DNA is widely considered to be superior to all other types of forensic evidence. It is a valuable crime-solving tool that has led to the arrest of thousands of criminals and has virtually transformed the legal system. As prosecuting attorney and author George "Woody" Clark writes: "The power of DNA evidence . . . led proponents of the science to victories, to defeats, and, perhaps most important, to change."[20]

How Conclusive Is DNA Evidence in Solving Crimes?

66 **Whether fluid recovered from a victim of rape, hairs found clutched in the hand of a murder victim, or even chewing gum carelessly discarded by a burglar, DNA testing can routinely lead to the identification of the person who left that evidence.** 99

—Janet Reno, foreword, to *Justice and Science: Trials and Triumphs of DNA Evidence,*
George "Woody" Clarke. New Brunswick, NJ: Rutgers University Press, 2008.

Reno is a former attorney general of the United States.

66 **DNA evidence is fallible on its own (although it is much more reliable than most other forensic evidence) and also as fallible as the humans who collect it and analyze it and interpret it. Which is to say, pretty fallible.** 99

—Effect Measure, "Solving a Crime Wave with DNA," March 27, 2009. http://scienceblogs.com.

The editors of Effect Measure are all senior public health scientists and practitioners.

* Editor's Note: While the definition of a primary source can be narrowly or broadly defined, for the purposes of Compact Research, a primary source consists of: 1) results of original research presented by an organization or researcher; 2) eyewitness accounts of events, personal experience, or work experience; 3) first-person editorials offering pundits' opinions; 4) government officials presenting political plans and/or policies; 5) representatives of organizations presenting testimony or policy.

"Modern DNA testing can provide powerful new evidence unlike anything known before."

> —John Roberts, *District Attorney's Office for the Third Judicial District et al. v. Osborne,"* June 18, 2009. www.supremecourtus.gov.

Roberts is the chief justice of the U.S. Supreme Court.

....

"Several years ago, Chicago did a study of eight convicted felons and their criminal histories. The results were sobering. Had DNA been collected at the time of the first felony arrest, 60 violent crimes committed by these offenders after their first arrest could have been prevented."

> —Gerald Bailey, "DNA Can Prevent Crime," *Miami Herald*, June 29, 2009. www.miamiherald.com.

Bailey is the commissioner of the Florida Department of Law Enforcement.

....

"The simple reality is that the interpretation of forensic evidence is not always based on scientific studies to determine its validity. This is a serious problem."

> —National Research Council of the National Academies, *Strengthening Forensic Science in the United States: A Path Forward.* Washington: National Academies Press, 2009. http://books.nap.edu.

An agency of the National Academy of Sciences, the National Research Council's mission is to improve government decision making and public policy and increase public awareness in the fields of science, engineering, technology, and health.

....

66 DNA evidence is both powerful and fragile. With the right approach and careful attention to how we process and handle this important evidence, we can use DNA to build the kind of cases that will hold up in court. 99

—Dick Warrington, "Who Says You Can't Do That? DNA Collection and Packaging," *Forensic*, April/May 2009. www.forensicmag.com.

Warrington is a crime scene consultant and training instructor.

66 Josiah Sutton served four and a half years for rape after the Houston Crime Lab tied him to crime-scene DNA. The lab was later found to be rife with problems, including a leaky roof that let rainwater contaminate evidence. 99

—Roger Koppl, "What's Wrong with CSI?" *Forbes*, June 2, 2008. www.forbes.com.

Koppl is a professor of economics and finance at Fairleigh Dickinson University's Silberman College of Business and a director of the Institute for Forensic Science Administration.

66 The conclusion that a DNA match proves the defendant's guilt is based primarily on the assumption that the probability against one individual's DNA matching another's is in the hundreds of millions, or even billions, depending on who is crunching the numbers. 99

—Reeves Law Group, "DNA Evidence: It's in Your Genes," FindLaw, 2007. http://criminal.findlaw.com.

Reeves Law Group is a criminal defense attorney practice in Grand Rapids, Michigan.

How Conclusive Is DNA Evidence in Solving Crimes?

- According to a 2008 report commissioned by the U.S. Department of Justice, the likelihood that any two nonidentical siblings have the same DNA profile is as little as **1 in 1 billion or more**.

- Studies have shown that DNA evidence is **far more effective** in solving crimes than eyewitness testimony, which is accurate only about half the time.

- Of the first **239 wrongfully convicted people** who were exonerated by DNA evidence, **78** had been convicted due to eyewitness testimony, and **99 percent** of those were either African American or Hispanic.

- Studies have shown that DNA is at least **five times as likely** to result in suspect identification compared to fingerprints.

- According to the Justice Project, which works to increase fairness and accuracy in America's criminal justice system, DNA is the most reliable and accurate type of evidence, but it can be gathered at only a **fraction of crime sciences**.

- DNA is most frequently used to solve **rape and murder cases** because biological evidence is more likely to be left at the crime scene.

- All 50 U.S. states have laws that require convicted **sex offenders** to submit DNA samples, and the majority have laws that require all **convicted felons** to submit DNA.

Sources of DNA Evidence

When evidence is collected at a crime scene, DNA may be collected from a number of sources. This chart provides a breakdown of various types of evidence, as well as the samples (sources) where DNA is typically found.

Evidence Collected from Crime Scene	Possible Location of DNA on the Evidence	Source of DNA
baseball bat or similar weapon	handle, end	sweat, skin, blood, tissue
hat, bandanna, or mask	inside	sweat, hair, dandruff
eyeglasses	nose or ear pieces, lens	sweat, skin
facial tissue, cotton swab	surface area	mucus, blood, sweat, semen, ear wax
dirty laundry	surface area	blood, sweat, semen
toothpick	tips	saliva
used cigarette	cigarette butt	saliva
stamp or envelope	licked area	saliva
tape or literature	inside/outside surface	skin, sweat
bottle, can, or glass	sides, mouthpiece	saliva, sweat
used condom	inside/outside/ surface	semen, vaginal or rectal cells
blanket, pillow, sheet	surface area	sweat, hair, semen, urine, saliva
"through and through" bullet	outside surface	blood, tissue
bite mark	person's skin or clothing	saliva
fingernail, partial fingernail	scrapings	blood, sweat, tissue

Source: DNA Initiative, "Identifying DNA Evidence." www.dna.gov.

- A report released in September 2009 by the National Research Council showed that **one out of every five** crime labs in the United States does not meet accreditation standards set by the National Academy of Crime Lab Directors.

- According to a 2008 report by the Urban Institute, the principal crimes investigated using DNA evidence—murder and rape—accounted for about **110,000** crimes in the United States during 2006. That same year there were more than **2 million** burglaries, and using DNA technology to solve such a high number of crimes is cost-prohibitive for many law enforcement agencies.

Funding for DNA Programs

In order to increase the availability of DNA technology to law enforcement agencies throughout the United States, as well as defray the additional cost, in 2004 the U.S. Department of Justice implemented a $1 billion five-year DNA initiative. Its goals are to reduce casework and crime lab backlogs, fund research and development, improve crime lab capacity, and provide training in DNA evidence. This graph show the various programs that these funds help pay for.

U.S. Department of Justice DNA Programs and Funding – 2007

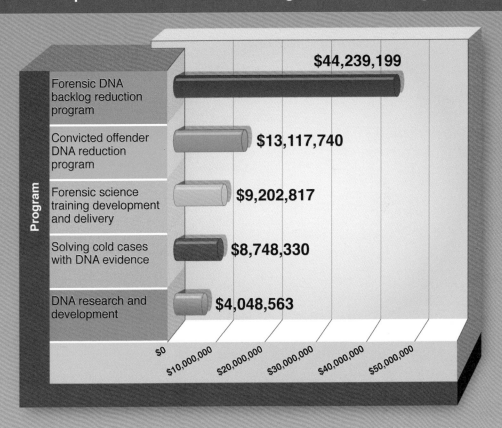

Source: U.S. Department of Justice, *Audit of the Convicted Offender DNA Backlog Reduction Program*, March 2009; www.usdoj.gov.

The Process of DNA Analysis

After a crime has been committed, investigators gather evidence at the scene and send it to a forensic crime lab for testing. If the evidence is shown to contain DNA, a process known as polymerase chain reaction is often used by lab technicians to replicate (amplify) the DNA in a test tube. According to the DNA Initiative, this process can result in millions of exact copies of DNA from samples as small as a few skin cells. This illustration shows the process the lab goes through when analyzing evidence for DNA.

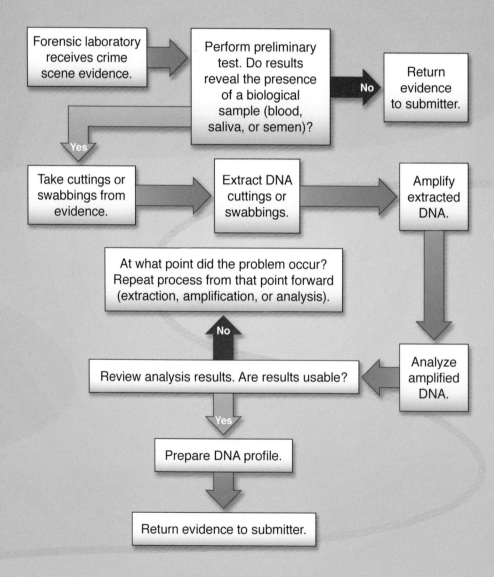

Source: U.S. Department of Justice, "The FBI DNA Laboratory: A Review of Protocol and Practice Vulnerabilities: Chapter Two: The Analysis of DNA," May 2004. www.usdoj.gov.

How Effective Is DNA Testing for Correcting Justice System Errors?

> **❝DNA testing has an unparalleled ability to exonerate the wrongfully convicted as well as to identify the guilty.❞**
>
> —Eric Holder, U.S. attorney general.

> **❝While DNA evidence does not always conclusively [exonerate] a defendant who alleges he was wrongfully convicted, it often points to the possibility that someone else may have committed the crime.❞**
>
> —Billy Wayne Sinclair, who spent 40 years in prison for unpremeditated murder and who is now a criminal defense paralegal and author.

As valuable as DNA evidence has become for connecting criminals with crimes, it is equally valuable for exonerating those who have been accused or convicted of crimes they did not commit. By analyzing DNA samples taken from a crime scene, investigators can determine whether it matches the DNA of a suspect. If it does not, police have likely arrested the wrong person, and they can begin hunting for the real perpetrator. This occurred in February 2006 after a man robbed a bar in West Palm Beach, Florida. In a photo lineup 2 witnesses identified Cody Davis as the robber, and police arrested him. When searching the crime scene, officers found a ski mask but did not give it much consideration because none of the eyewitnesses said that the robber had been wearing a mask. Although it was turned over to the crime lab for DNA testing, it was not treated as a priority. Davis went to trial and was convicted and sentenced to 3 years in prison. Four months later the crime lab completed testing on the ski mask and found that the DNA did not match

Davis. It did, however, match the DNA of Jeremy Prichard, who was in jail awaiting trial on different charges. Detectives questioned Prichard, and he confessed to the February robbery, as well as 3 others.

The district attorney's office immediately moved to have Davis's conviction overturned, and he was released from prison in early 2007. According to former prosecutor Sean Sweeney, this case illustrates the unreliability of eyewitness testimony. He writes: "Eyewitness testimony is among the most subjective and inherently fallible types of evidence utilized in any criminal trial."[21]

Studying Wrongful Convictions

As of September 2009, 242 wrongfully convicted people had been exonerated through DNA evidence, including 17 who had been sentenced to death. How many others may have been convicted of crimes they did not commit is unknown. Although DNA evidence has vastly improved law enforcement's ability to separate the guilty from the innocent, it can only be obtained from a small number of crime scenes. According to Peter Neufeld, cofounder of the Innocence Project, DNA samples are available in fewer than 10 percent of violent crimes, which means that most cases still rely on eyewitness testimony and other forensic evidence. Neufeld adds that there are likely thousands of innocent people who have been wrongfully convicted, due in large part to the lack of DNA evidence.

> As valuable as DNA evidence has become for connecting criminals with crimes, it is equally valuable for exonerating those who have been accused or convicted of crimes they did not commit.

In a study published in 2007, law professors from the University of Michigan and Michigan State concurred with Neufeld's theory. They caution that "exonerations are highly unrepresentative of wrongful convictions in general. The main thing we can safely conclude from exonerations is that there are many other false convictions that we have not discovered."[22] Another study, called "Judging Innocence," was published in

January 2008 by Brandon L. Garrett, a law professor at the University of Virginia. Garrett examined 200 cases of prisoners who had been wrongfully convicted between 1989 and 2007 and were later released based on DNA evidence. He found that nearly 80 percent of the time, they had been erroneously identified by eyewitnesses, and in one-fourth of those cases, eyewitness testimony was the only evidence against the accused. In 57 percent of the cases, flawed forensic evidence was involved, such as blood, semen, and/or microscopic hair comparison, which Garrett calls "notoriously unreliable. Absent any data regarding probabilities that hair or fiber may match visually, experts can make only a subjective assessment whether two hairs or two fibers are 'consistent and share similarities.'"[23]

During his study Garrett also discovered that informants, including some who were incarcerated, testified against the wrongfully accused in 18 percent of the cases. "Particularly disturbing," he writes, "were three cases in which the codefendant, cooperating witness, or informant had ulterior motives beyond seeking special treatment from law enforcement: DNA testing later revealed that they were the actual perpetrators."[24]

Also, 16 percent of the accused were convicted due to false confessions—and nearly two-thirds were juveniles, mentally retarded, or both. Garrett explains why DNA technology must be pursued as aggressively as possible: "DNA testing provides the most accurate and powerful scientific proxy available to establish biological identity. It sets the 'gold standard' for other forms of forensic analysis." Later in the report Garrett says that the U.S. criminal justice system needs to make it a priority to judge guilt or innocence more accurately. "Additional studies should be undertaken to examine the growing number of DNA exonerations, so that future efforts to reform our criminal system benefit from the lessons that we now can learn about how to better judge innocence."[25]

> **Although DNA evidence has vastly improved law enforcement's ability to separate the guilty from the innocent, it can only be obtained from a small number of crime scenes.**

The Correlation Between Justice and Wealth

As the exoneration of 242 prisoners illustrates, DNA has the ability to clear those who have been wrongfully convicted and/or imprisoned. Yet in numerous cases DNA evidence may be available, but testing and analysis are not done because of the high cost. Most people accused of crimes do not have the financial means to hire a private attorney, so they are represented by public defenders. The U.S. Department of Justice states that two out of three people charged with felonies at the federal level cannot afford an attorney, and the number is even higher in state courts. According to Radley Balko, who is a former policy analyst with the Cato Institute and senior editor for *Reason* magazine, public defenders are often not able to provide the type of defense that could potentially exonerate their clients through DNA evidence. "Indigent defendants don't have their own forensics experts or private investigators," he writes, "and courts aren't always obliged to grant them taxpayer money to hire them." Balko adds that underfunding, combined with mandatory minimum sentences and an overall increase in the number of crimes, "results in an overwhelming high number of plea-bargained admissions of guilt, as prosecutors look to pad conviction rates and defense attorneys have no choice but to slough off burdensome caseloads."[26]

> In numerous cases DNA evidence may be available, but testing and analysis are not done because of the high cost.

The importance of one's ability to afford excellent attorneys who persuade courts to enter DNA evidence became apparent in April 2007. That month, 3 lacrosse players from Duke University were declared innocent of a rape for which they had been indicted the previous year. A woman accused the men of gang-raping her in a home on campus. The 3 adamantly denied that they had ever touched her, but prosecutor Mike Nifong aggressively pursued their conviction—even though the men's DNA was not found anywhere on the woman's body. The 3 were all from wealthy families, so they were able to hire top-rated attorneys who worked for more than a year on their case and secured DNA tests. Finally, 395 days after they were arrested, North Carolina's attorney general announced that DNA evidence had cleared them and all charges were dropped. After the announcement was made, Reade Seligmann, one of the accused, spoke about the legal representation that had contributed to the ruling: "I can't imagine what they do to people who don't have the resources to defend themselves."[27]

Evidence Preservation

It has been proved time and time again that when DNA evidence exists, it can help save innocent people from being convicted and exonerate those who have been convicted and imprisoned for crimes they did not commit. But DNA is not available at most crime scenes, and even when it is, it is not always preserved once a conviction has taken place and the case is closed. According to an August 2008 report by the Justice Project, all but 12 states and the District of Columbia lack statutes requiring that evidence be preserved throughout an inmate's incarceration. "Even in states with such statutes on the books," the group writes, "rules regarding the preservation of evidence are often ignored. In New York City, for example, despite the support of prosecutors for post-conviction DNA testing, such testing did not happen in several cases because evidence had been lost."[28] The same report discusses Kevin Byrd, who spent 12 years in prison after being convicted of rape. He was exonerated after DNA showed that he could not have been the rapist—but he almost lost the chance to have his DNA tested. An investigation showed that the crime lab had destroyed 50 old rape kits that were in storage, and the one that later exonerated Byrd was among those scheduled for destruction. "Whether due to a filing error or an unknown party's intentional intervention," writes the Justice Project, "his evidence was saved, and it proved his innocence. Statutes requiring preservation of evidence would significantly expand opportunities to correct otherwise irreversible errors."[29]

> It has been proved time and time again that when DNA evidence exists, it can help save innocent people from being convicted and exonerate those who have been convicted and imprisoned for crimes they did not commit.

An Escape from Death

Shortly after his seventeenth birthday in 1997, Ryan Matthews was arrested for robbing a convenience store and murdering the owner. Eyewitnesses said that the killer wore a ski mask and described him as being shorter than Matthews. Yet Matthews became the prime suspect. DNA testing was done, but according to the Innocence Project, Matthews's court-appointed attorney was unprepared and unable to handle the evidence. At his 1999 trial the jury found Matthews guilty, and the judge sentenced him to die by lethal injection.

> There is no way of knowing for sure how many wrongfully accused prisoners die while they are incarcerated.

After Matthews had spent four years on death row, a team of attorneys had the ski mask retested. The DNA results excluded Matthews and matched the profile of a prisoner who was serving time for another murder that happened a few months after the convenience store owner had been killed. In 2004 Matthews was released from prison and exonerated of the crime. "I really didn't know whether he would be eventually absolved of the crime," says his mother, Pauline Matthews, "but I always knew that Ryan was innocent. I always believed in my heart that he was innocent."[30]

An Exoneration That Came Too Late

There is no way of knowing for sure how many wrongfully accused prisoners die while they are incarcerated. One case that was widely publicized involved Timothy Cole, who had been convicted of the 1985 rape of Michele Mallin, then a 20-year-old student at Texas Tech University. Mallin told police officers that just before the assault, she had been walking to her car in a parking lot when she was approached by a man asking if she had jumper cables. She said he grabbed her neck and put her in a choke hold, and then threatened her with a knife. He forced his way into her car and drove her to the outskirts of town, where he raped her.

The next day Mallin looked at pictures of possible suspects and selected Cole as her attacker, and she also identified him in a police lineup. Cole was arrested and charged with Mallin's rape. Although he was offered a plea bargain deal that would have given him probation rather than prison, he refused. Accepting the deal meant that he would have to plead guilty, and he would not do so because he steadfastly maintained his innocence. Cole was eventually tried in a Lubbock, Texas, court, convicted, and sentenced to 25 years in prison.

In 2007 a man named Jerry Johnson sent a letter to Cole's family home addressed to Cole, and in it he confessed that it was he who had raped Mallin. Johnson wrote:

> I have been trying to locate you since 1995 to tell you I wish to confess I did in fact commit the rape Lubbock wrongly convicted you of. It is very possible that through a written confession from me and DNA testing, you can finally have your name cleared of the rape . . . if this letter reaches you, please contact me by writing so that we can arrange to take the steps to get the process started. Whatever it takes, I will do it.[31]

The letter never reached Cole, however. At the age of 39, he had died in prison 8 years before from complications related to a severe asthma attack. Despite his death, the case was reopened. New DNA evidence confirmed Cole's innocence and he was exonerated posthumously.

Triumphs and Challenges

DNA evidence has proved to be as effective in clearing the wrongly accused as it is in identifying criminals. As a February 2009 editorial in the *Seattle Times* states: "DNA is a tool of detection and exoneration—both to the benefit of the public."[32] The more often DNA is used to investigate crimes, the more valuable it will become. But there are challenges, due to additional cost for DNA analysis, evidence contamination at the crime scene, and preservation of evidence. If those problems are eventually overcome, it is probable that fewer people will end up in prison for crimes they did not commit.

How Effective Is DNA Testing for Correcting Justice System Errors?

66 **There is no doubt that DNA evidence has been pivotal in preventing many wrongfully convicted people from being executed.** 99

—Effect Measure, "Solving a Crime Wave with DNA," March 27, 2009. http://scienceblogs.com.

The editors of Effect Measure are all senior public health scientists and practitioners.

66 **Although best known for clearing the wrongfully convicted, DNA evidence has on occasion linked innocent people to crimes. In the lab, it can be contaminated or mislabeled; samples can be switched. In the courtroom, its significance has often been overstated by lawyers or misunderstood by jurors.** 99

—Maura Dolan and Jason Felch, "The Danger of DNA: It Isn't Perfect," *Los Angeles Times*, December 26, 2008. www.latimes.com.

Dolan is a legal affairs writer and Felch is an investigative reporter for the *Los Angeles Times* newspaper.

* Editor's Note: While the definition of a primary source can be narrowly or broadly defined, for the purposes of Compact Research, a primary source consists of: 1) results of original research presented by an organization or researcher; 2) eyewitness accounts of events, personal experience, or work experience; 3) first-person editorials offering pundits' opinions; 4) government officials presenting political plans and/or policies; 5) representatives of organizations presenting testimony or policy.

"DNA exonerations have called into question the accuracy of ballistics analysis, bite mark evidence, hair and carpet fiber evidence, shoe print analysis, jailhouse informants, and even fingerprint identification, once the gold standard of the forensics world."

—Radley Balko, "Eyewitness Testimony on Trial," *Reason*, April 8, 2009. www.reason.com.

Balko is a former policy analyst with the Cato Institute and is now senior editor for *Reason* magazine.

"Nobody knows how many innocent people are in prison, but we do know that the DNA exonerations are just the tip of the iceberg."

—John Grisham, "Lessons Not Learned," Innocence Project, June 8, 2009. www.innocenceproject.org.

Grisham, a former criminal law attorney, is a best-selling author of suspense fiction and a member of the Innocence Project's board of directors.

"DNA exonerations cannot solve the serious problems that clearly exist in our criminal justice system. . . . But they do illuminate the need for serious reform within the criminal justice system."

—Amnesty International, "DNA Evidence Won't Save Innocent People from Death Penalty," Opposing Views, February 18, 2009. www.opposingviews.com.

Amnesty International is a worldwide movement of people who campaign for internationally recognized human rights for all.

❝Without post-conviction DNA testing, it is likely that the more than two-hundred DNA exonerees would still be in prison today.❞

> —The Justice Project, *Improving Access to Post-Conviction DNA Testing*, August 12, 2008. www.thejusticeproject.org.

The Justice Project works to fight injustice and increase fairness and accuracy in the criminal justice system.

❝To point out the obvious—the application of DNA technology to postconviction appeals has compelled more than a few changes to the U.S. criminal justice system. . . . Today, the vast majority of states recognize the power of DNA to determine actual innocence years after other forensic evidence has proven flawed.❞

> —Chris Asplen, "The DNA Connection: Postconviction DNA Testing: An International Impact," *Forensic*, April/May 2008. www.forensicmag.com.

Asplen is a former U.S. assistant district attorney and prosecutor who specializes in the prosecution of sex crimes and child abuse.

❝Since the inception of DNA evidence, more than 220 criminal defendants in the United States have been exonerated because their DNA shows that they were not the individual that committed the crime for which they were convicted. More than 75% of these false convictions were based on faulty eyewitness identifications.❞

> —Travis Tormey, "The System Makes Mistakes: Eyewitness Identifications and DNA Evidence," *New Jersey Criminal Defense Journal*, March 9, 2009. www.njcriminaldefensejournal.com.

Tormey is a criminal defense attorney from Redbank, New Jersey.

Facts and Illustrations

How Effective Is DNA Testing for Correcting Justice System Errors?

- The Justice Project states that the vast majority of **DNA exonerations** involve **sexual assault** cases where biological evidence is often present with the potential clearly to indicate guilt.

- Only about **50 percent** of the U.S. states have legislation in place that mandates the automatic preservation of evidence upon conviction of a defendant.

- As of September 2009 DNA tests had exonerated **242 prisoners** who were convicted of murder.

- Seventeen of the prisoners who have been exonerated for murder were on **death row**.

- Of the 242 wrongfully convicted people who have been exonerated and released from prison, **Texas** had the highest number at 38 followed by **Illinois** at 29.

- In 1993 **Kirk Bloodsworth** became the first death row prisoner to be exonerated by DNA evidence.

- The Innocence Project states that exonerations have been won in 33 states and Washington, D.C.; since 2000 there have been **172 exonerations**.

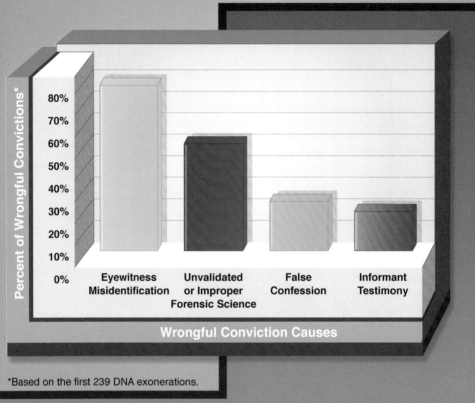

Exonerating the Wrongfully Convicted

According to the Innocence Project, as of September 2009, 242 wrongfully convicted people had been exonerated and released from prison, including 17 who were on death row. Although different types of evidence were involved, most of the convictions were based on eyewitness misidentification.

Percent of Wrongful Convictions*

80%
70%
60%
50%
40%
30%
20%
10%
0%

| Eyewitness Misidentification | Unvalidated or Improper Forensic Science | False Confession | Informant Testimony |

Wrongful Conviction Causes

*Based on the first 239 DNA exonerations.

Note: Some of the accused were convicted based on more than one type of evidence.

Source: John Grisham, Revaluating Lineups: *Why Witnesses Make Mistakes and How to Reduce the Chance of a Misidentification*, Innocence Project, July 16, 2009.

- Of the 242 prisoners who have been exonerated by DNA evidence, **144 were African American**, 70 were Caucasian, 21 were Latino, and 2 were Asian American; race is unknown in the other 5.

- According to the Innocence Project, **75 percent** of the prisoners who were wrongfully convicted had been misidentified by eyewitnesses, and nearly half involved misidentification by multiple eye-witnesses.

- An estimated **25 percent** of wrongful convictions overturned by DNA evidence involved a false confession or admission by the accused.

- A July 2009 report by the Innocence Project states that in **36 percent** of the witness misidentifications that led to innocent people spending time in prison, the real perpetrator was identified through DNA evidence.

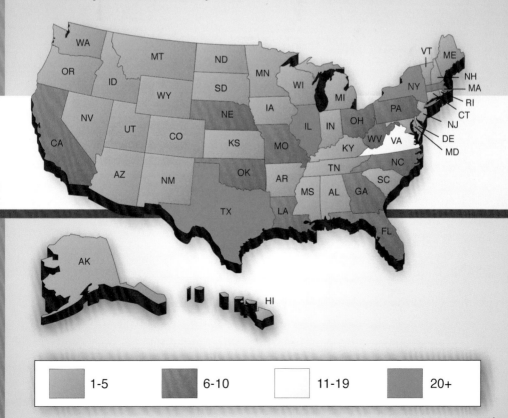

Exonerations by State

Of the 242 wrongfully convicted people who where exonerated and released from prison as of September 2009, the highest number, 38, was from Texas followed by Illinois at 29. Every state had at least 1 exoneration.

1-5   6-10   11-19   20+

Source: Innocence Project, "Exonerations by State," August 2009. www.innocenceproject.org.

Preservation of Evidence

DNA evidence has proven its value in reversing wrongful convictions, but this can only occur when evidence has been preserved. Although most states have at least some legislation in place to prohibit destruction of evidence after a conviction has been obtained, 18 states have no such legislation.

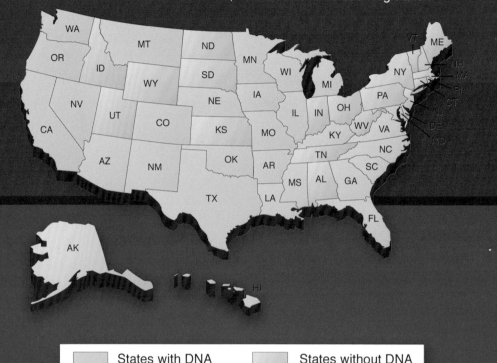

States with DNA preservation laws

States without DNA preservation laws

Source: Innocence Project, "Reforms by State," 2009. www.innocenceproject.org.

- Dallas County, **Texas**, has the **highest exoneration** rate in the United States.

- The Innocence Project closes cases each year for various reasons, such as no biological evidence being available. **Twenty-two percent** of cases that have been closed since 2004 were closed because of missing evidence.

Should Prisoners Have a Right to DNA Testing?

> 66 Over two hundred years ago, the framers of the Constitution could obviously never have foreseen the arrival of DNA testing. Had they been able to, it's unthinkable that they would not have guaranteed a man the scientific chance to prove his own innocence. 99
>
> —William Kickham, a criminal defense attorney from Boston, Massachusetts.

> 66 Given the backlog existing in many DNA testing labs, a [Supreme Court] decision that prisoners had a right to have DNA tests performed might have created a huge priority conflict between pending cases and closed cases. 99
>
> —Paul Bergman, a law professor at the University of California–Los Angeles School of Law.

In January 2009 attorneys with the Innocence Project filed a brief with the U.S. Supreme Court on behalf of a prisoner named William Osborne. A resident of Anchorage, Alaska, Osborne had been convicted in 1993 of rape and attempted murder and was sentenced to 26 years in prison. Maintaining his innocence, he had requested DNA testing on a number of occasions, but each time his request was denied. Osborne's lawyers argued that he should have access to DNA testing because the right to it was ensured for all citizens under the U.S. Constitution. They cited the Fourteenth Amendment, which forbids states from denying any person "life, liberty or property, without due process of law," nor can any state "deny to any person within its jurisdiction the equal protection of the laws."[33]

Osborne's case was one of the few that made it to the U.S. Supreme Court. In June 2009, in a five to four decision, the justices ruled against him, stating that convicted criminals do not have a constitutional right to DNA testing. Justice Samuel A. Alito concurred with the majority, writing: "Allowing Mr. Osborne . . . to forgo testing at trial and then request it from prison would allow prisoners to play games with the criminal justice system. After conviction, with nothing to lose, the defendant could demand DNA testing in the hope that some happy accident—for example, degradation or contamination of the evidence—would provide the basis for seeking postconviction relief."[34]

> " Alaska is one of only three states . . . that have no legislation in place to give prisoners the right to DNA testing. "

John Paul Stevens was one of the four justices who dissented from the majority decision. Stevens expressed the view that Osborne was entitled to DNA testing. "Osborne has demonstrated a constitutionally protected right to due process which the State of Alaska thus far has not vindicated and which this Court is both empowered and obliged to safeguard," Stevens wrote. "On the record before us, there is no reason to deny access to the evidence and there are many reasons to provide it, not least of which is a fundamental concern in ensuring that justice has been done in this case."[35]

States Decide

As a result of the Supreme Court ruling in the Osborne case, it is up to the states to decide whether convicted offenders have the right to a DNA test. Alaska is one of only three states (the other two being Massachusetts and Oklahoma) that have no legislation in place to give prisoners the right to DNA testing. That is why the test was repeatedly denied to Osborne long before his case ever reached the Supreme Court. Even though the Innocence Project offered to pay for the test, officials still refused. Robert Morgenthau, a prosecuting attorney from New York City, says that Alaska fought "tooth and nail" to deny Osborne access to a DNA test, and says he is "mystified" by the prosecutors' steadfast refusal to allow him to be tested. "Not every defendant can fairly claim entitlement to post-trial forensic testing," Morgenthau writes. "But when a defendant who has always protested innocence will pay for a test that will resolve that protest one way or the other, only stubbornness can explain denying him access to the evidence. What can Alaska be afraid of—finding that it has imprisoned the wrong man?"[36]

Unlike in Alaska, prisoners in Pennsylvania who have been convicted of a capital crime and/or are awaiting execution may file a petition for DNA testing with the court. The legislation does not guarantee that the testing will be done, however, as it is still up to the court to decide whether to grant the request. If the court is not convinced that DNA evidence would prove the prisoner's innocence, the request will likely be denied.

This happened in April 2009 when Anthony Wright's request for DNA testing was being considered by the Pennsylvania Supreme Court. In June 1993 Wright had been convicted of the robbery, rape, and murder of an elderly woman in Philadelphia. In arguing against the DNA test, the prosecutor referred to evidence that he said clearly pointed toward Wright's guilt, including the testimony of four eyewitnesses and clothing stained with the victim's blood that police reportedly found at his home. The prosecutor said this was more than enough to prove that Wright was guilty. Assistant district attorney Peter Carr explains: "The evidence was so overwhelming at the time of trial that there was no reasonable possibility (the evidence) would exonerate the defendant, which is required by the law. If we agree to it here, we basically have to agree in every single case. That's not reasonable."[37]

> " Those who argue that all defendants should have the right to DNA testing say that it is the only way to prove definitively whether they did—or did not—commit a crime. "

Those who argue that all defendants should have the right to DNA testing say that it is the only way to prove definitively whether they did—or did not—commit a crime. One of the main reasons for their perspective is the number of innocent people who have been found guilty and imprisoned for crimes they did not commit. Often cited in support of this perspective are the 242 former prisoners who have been exonerated through DNA evidence. One wrongly convicted person who was exonerated by DNA is Alan Newton, who lives in the Bronx area of New York City. Newton spent 21 years in prison for rape, robbery, and assault. At the time of his arrest, he asked for a DNA test, but the request was denied because he was told the rape kit from the victim had been lost. In 2005 the Innocence Project became involved and pressured the district attorney's office to search for the rape kit, which was eventually located. After DNA was tested and showed that Newton was not the assailant, he was exonerated and released from prison in July 2006.

> " Even though DNA has been shown to be the most reliable type of evidence, using it to investigate *all* crimes where evidence is available is not affordable for many law enforcement agencies. "

Cost Issues

One major challenge with expanding DNA testing for everyone who has been accused of a crime, as well as those who have been convicted, is the high cost. Even though DNA has been shown to be the most reliable type of evidence, using it to investigate *all* crimes where evidence is available is not affordable for many law enforcement agencies. As an April 2008 study by the Urban Institute explains:

> Our research suggests that large numbers of offenders not currently identified by traditional investigations could be identified via DNA. A gap arises because the capacity of police and labs to identify and collect DNA is limited, crime laboratories are severely constrained in their ability to process biological evidence in volume, and prosecutors have not prepared for the impact of large numbers of cases where DNA evidence is the primary source of offender identification.[38]

The study found that cost is a major consideration when using DNA evidence to investigate property crimes such as robbery and burglary. The authors state that identifying and arresting suspects who would not have been caught via traditional investigations adds an extra $4,500 per suspect to the case. The cost is even higher if the suspect is arrested, which adds another $14,000 for each additional arrest. If the case is accepted for prosecution, it costs another $6,200.

Cost has become a serious issue at the Los Angeles County Sheriff's Department—so much so that in June 2009 officials announced that they were suspending DNA testing on more than 4,000 rape kits that were already in storage. In 2008 the Los Angeles chief of police had stated that the department would test for DNA in all rape cases, but it was not long before the department discovered their financial resources were not adequate to do that. This prompted the decision to suspend testing on the older rape kits and instead focus resources on current cases.

Crime Lab Backlogs

Expanding DNA testing to all suspects is also a challenge because of the backlog of evidence in crime labs. As DNA collection has increased, the labs have become more and more backlogged. According to a March 2009 report by the U.S. Department of Justice, the national backlog of DNA samples was 708,706 in 2007, although this was a decrease from more than 1.1 million in 2005. Kellie Greene is a rape victim who was affected by a crime lab backlog. She waited 3 years for the lab to test DNA that the man who assaulted her left on her leggings—and when the test finally identified who he was, she was horrified to learn that he had committed an earlier rape and the DNA from that case was backlogged for 2 years. "Had they been able to test the DNA in that earlier case," she says, "my rape would have never happened."[39]

> " According to a March 2009 report by the U.S Department of Justice, the national backlog of DNA samples was 708,706 in 2007, although this was a decrease from more than 1.1 million in 2005. "

Greene's experience is not uncommon. After a legal secretary was raped in her Los Angeles home, the detective took the rape kit to the crime lab and was told that it would take more than a year for the testing to take place. Suspecting that her attacker was a repeat offender who would strike again, the detective drove 350 miles to Sacramento, where the backlog was not as bad. It still took four months for the DNA to be tested, and when the test came back, there was a match in a database of previous offenders. "Yet in the months while the rape kit sat on a shelf," writes columnist Nicholas D. Kristof, "the suspect had allegedly struck twice more. Police said he broke into the homes of a pregnant woman and a 17-year-old girl, sexually assaulting each of them."[40]

Crime lab backlogs are a problem all over the United States. In 2007 the *Los Angeles Times* reported that the city's police department had nearly 7,000 untested DNA samples from sexual assault cases in cold storage. One investigation by journalists from *ProPublica* found that during 2005, backlogs in crime labs across the country nearly doubled. The article reports that the California Department of Justice alone has a backlog of more than 53,500 DNA samples, all of which await testing.

> **California's legislation also calls for DNA evidence to be preserved during the entire time a prisoner is incarcerated; he or she may request testing no matter what the original plea was, and the court provides a state-funded test if the prisoner cannot afford it.**

A Topic of Debate

Whether all suspects and convicted offenders should be entitled to DNA testing is a controversial issue. Should taxpayers pay for all who are accused of a crime to have DNA testing? Some say yes, others say no. As for postconviction DNA testing, opinions are sharply divided. Laws differ from state to state, and many prosecutors insist that such testing should not be available to all prisoners. Advocacy groups such as the Justice

Project and Innocence Project disagree, arguing that they should. John Terzano, president of the Justice Project, writes:

> States should . . . ensure that all inmates with a DNA-based innocence claim may petition for DNA testing at any time without regard to plea, confession, self-implication, the nature of the crime, or previous unfavorable test results. . . . And because DNA testing technology continues to improve, a defendant's right to request testing must not be subject to time limitations. If new technology develops that might change the outcome of a test, the test should be performed.[41]

In its August 2008 report, *Increasing Access to Post-Conviction DNA Testing: A Policy Review*, the Justice Project addresses the problems that currently exist with DNA testing and suggests solutions to overcome them. One recommendation is that states enact laws requiring "the most expansive use of DNA evidence possible. States with post-conviction DNA testing statutes that create barriers to accessibility of such evidence should revise their laws."[42]

The report highlights states that have expanded their postconviction DNA laws and says that other states should do the same. For instance, Florida imposes no time limitations for prisoners to petition for DNA tests and requires preservation of evidence throughout a defendant's entire sentence. Also, even those who initially pled guilty may request testing, and the state pays for DNA testing if the petitioner cannot afford it. Another state that the Justice Project cites in its report is California, which it says has a "model post-conviction DNA testing statute."[43] Like Florida, California has legislation that calls for DNA evidence to be preserved during the entire time a prisoner is incarcerated; he or she may request testing no matter what the original plea was, and the court provides a state-funded test if the prisoner cannot afford it.

Can This Be Resolved?

DNA testing is a powerful law enforcement tool that has resulted in numerous arrests and convictions, as well as the exoneration of hundreds of people who have been wrongfully accused and/or convicted. But making DNA tests available to *all* suspects and convicted offenders presents numerous challenges. Collecting and analyzing DNA evidence adds significant costs to each case and also contributes to serious crime lab backlogs. By far the greatest controversy is over whether postconviction testing should be available to all prisoners who request it, with many prosecutors saying it is unnecessary and others arguing that it should be every prisoner's right. So will the two sides ever come to an agreement? No one can answer that question with any certainty.

Should Prisoners Have a Right to DNA Testing?

"In ruling that inmates have no right to sophisticated DNA evidence that could exonerate them, five conservative Supreme Court justices have taken a cruelly cramped view of the protections of the Bill of Rights."

—*Los Angeles Times* editorial staff, "The Supreme Court Ruling: Wrong on Rights," June 19, 2009.

The *Los Angeles Times* is the second-largest metropolitan daily newspaper in the United States.

"This case is not a case about doing justice. It's really about the latest attempt to give convicted criminals yet another bite at the apple . . . and another opportunity to bog down the justice system with more frivolous appeals over evidence that's already been played out. Understanding that, the Court got it right."

—Andrew M. Grossman, "Understanding *Osborne* and Access to DNA Evidence," Heritage Foundation, June 18, 2009. http://blog.heritage.org.

Grossman is a senior legal policy analyst with the Center for Legal and Judicial Studies.

* Editor's Note: While the definition of a primary source can be narrowly or broadly defined, for the purposes of Compact Research, a primary source consists of: 1) results of original research presented by an organization or researcher; 2) eyewitness accounts of events, personal experience, or work experience; 3) first-person editorials offering pundits' opinions; 4) government officials presenting political plans and/or policies; 5) representatives of organizations presenting testimony or policy.

Primary Source Quotes

> ❝ **Post-conviction DNA testing provides an outlet—often the only outlet—through which defendants can prove their innocence.** ❞

—The Justice Project, *Improving Access to Post-Conviction DNA Testing*, August 12, 2008. www.thejusticeproject.org.

The Justice Project works to fight injustice and increase fairness and accuracy in the criminal justice system.

> ❝ **In a nation that prides itself on the rule of law, there is no good reason to deny prisoners the right to DNA testing if it can prove their innocence, identify the guilty and prevent a tragic miscarriage of justice.** ❞

—Marc H. Morial, "DNA Testing Should Be a Right!" *To Be Equal*, March 18, 2009. www.nul.org.

Morial is president and chief executive officer of the National Urban League.

> ❝ **The sad truth is that it often takes a series of miracles to gain access to post-conviction DNA testing.** ❞

—John Terzano, "Post-Conviction DNA Testing Shouldn't Depend on Miracles," *Huffington Post*, August 12, 2008. www.huffingtonpost.com.

Terzano is president of the Justice Project, an organization that works to increase fairness and accuracy in the criminal justice system.

66 The increased demand for DNA analyses, without a corresponding growth in forensic laboratory capacity, has caused a large backlog of unanalyzed DNA samples from convicted offenders and crime scenes, and this backlog can significantly delay criminal investigations. 99

—U.S. Department of Justice, *Audit of the Convicted Offender DNA Backlog Reduction Program*, March 2008. www.usdoj.gov.

The U.S. Department of Justice is charged with enforcing U.S. law, ensuring public safety, providing federal leadership in preventing and controlling crime, and ensuring fair and impartial administration of justice for Americans.

66 The Supreme Court's decision was an act of judicial restraint which limits their power and relies on precedent as opposed to judicial activism. Similar to death penalty statutes, the court deferred the decision to the state legislatures to determine how prisoners get access to DNA evidence. 99

—Randall Mayes, "Do We Have a Right to DNA Evidence in Trials?" Institute for Ethics & Emerging Technologies (IEET), June 20, 2009. http://ieet.org.

Mayes is a science writer, policy analyst, and IEET fellow.

66 The Supreme Court's willingness to turn a blind eye to wrongly convicted prisoners is troubling—particularly in light of the 240 exonerations through DNA since 1989. 99

—Marissa Bluestine and David Rudovsky, "DNA Tests Should Be Available to Prisoners," *Philadelphia Inquirer*, June 25, 2009. www.philly.com.

Bluestine is the legal director of the Pennsylvania Innocence Project, and Rudovsky is the vice president of its board.

❝The fact that nearly all the States have now recognized some postconviction right to DNA evidence makes it more, not less, appropriate to recognize a limited federal right to such evidence in cases where litigants are unfairly barred from obtaining relief in state court.❞

—John Paul Stevens, *District Attorney's Office for the Third Judicial District et al. v. Osborne,* June 18, 2009. www.supremecourtus.gov.

Stevens is a U.S. Supreme Court justice.

❝Federal law already guarantees access to DNA evidence held by the federal government under specific conditions, and I hope that all states will follow the federal government's lead on this issue.❞

—Eric Holder, "Remarks as Prepared for Delivery by Attorney General Eric Holder at the Vera Institute of Justice's Third Annual Justice Address," U.S. Department of Justice, July 9, 2009. www.justice.gov.

Holder is the attorney general of the United States.

Facts and Illustrations

Should Prisoners Have a Right to DNA Testing?

- In June 2009 the Supreme Court ruled that **DNA testing is not a guaranteed right** under the U.S. Constitution.

- Of the **242 post conviction DNA exonerations** as of September 2009, the actual perpetrator was identified in **more than 10** of the cases.

- An April 2008 study published by the Urban Institute found that identifying and arresting suspects who would not have been caught via traditional investigations adds an extra **$4,500 per suspect** to the case, ranging from a low of approximately $1,466 in Denver to an estimated $8,147 in Los Angeles.

- The most recent states to pass statutes allowing **postconviction DNA testing** were South Carolina and Wyoming in 2008 and South Dakota and Mississippi in 2009.

- Alabama and Kentucky only allow postconviction DNA testing in **capital cases**, or those that involve murder.

- Pennsylvania only allows postconviction DNA testing for **people who were convicted before 1995**, or in cases where DNA testing was not previously conducted.

- The three states that do not have any DNA access laws are **Alaska, Massachusetts,** and **Oklahoma**.

The Growth of CODIS

The FBI's Combined DNA Index System, called CODIS, is a central database that contains DNA profiles from laboratories throughout the United States. CODIS is a 3-tiered system with separate local, state, and national DNA databases. Since it was implemented in 1998, it has grown to hold more than 7 million offender profiles. This graph shows CODIS's growth from 2000 to 2009.

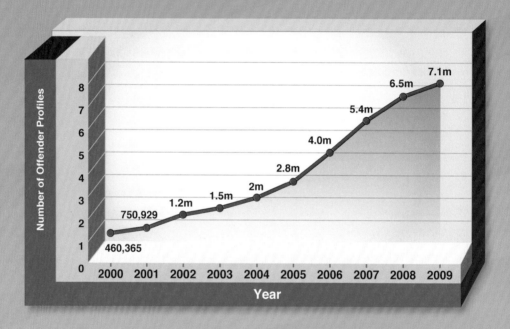

Sources: Federal Bureau of Investigation, "CODIS Combined DNA Index System," 2008. www.fbi.gov; "CODIA–NDIS Statistics," June 2009. www.fbi.gov.

- **Alaska** is the only U.S. state where there have been no known cases of prisoners being granted DNA testing through a court order or the consent of a prosecutor.

- The U.S. Department of Justice states that California has the highest number of crime lab backlogs, with **60,189 offender profiles** waiting to be tested as of March 2009.

- According to the Innocence Project, 27 states, the federal government, and the District of Columbia have passed laws to **financially compensate** people who have been wrongfully incarcerated.

- In **35 percent** of false confession or admission cases that resulted in wrongful convictions, the accused was 18 years old or younger and/or developmentally disabled.

- The Innocence Project states that the average age of exonorees at the time of their wrongful convictions was **26**.

Decades in Prison

The possibility of reversing a wrongful conviction is the strongest argument for greater access to DNA testing. The Innocence Project states that the 241 convicted offenders who have been exonerated as of August 2009 collectively served more than 3,000 years behind bars. This table shows the 14 prisoners who served the greatest amount of time in prison before being exonerated.

Name of Exonerated	State	Years Spent in Prison
William Dillon	Florida	27
Charles Chatman	Texas	26.5
Michael Evans	Illinois	26
Paul Terry	Illinois	26
Luis Diaz	Florida	25
Joseph Fears Jr.	Ohio	25
Rickie Johnson	Louisiana	25
Alan Crotzer	Florida	24.5
Jerry Miller	Illinois	24.5
Robert Clark	Georgia	23.5
Johnny Briscoe	Missouri	23
Wilton Dedge	Florida	22
Clark McMillan	Tennessee	22
Billy Wayne Miller	Texas	22

Source: Innocence Project, "Know the Cases: Browse the Profiles," 2009. www.innocenceproject.org.

DNA Database Backlogs

Crime labs throughout the United States are experiencing severe backlogs, especially where DNA testing and analysis is concerned. Allowing all prisoners access to DNA testing after conviction, regardless of the merits of their case, would add to that backlog. According to the U.S. Department of Justice, California had the worst backlog as of March 2009, closely followed by the state of Washington.

Convicted offender backlog as reported to the U.S. Department of Justice's Office of the Inspector General

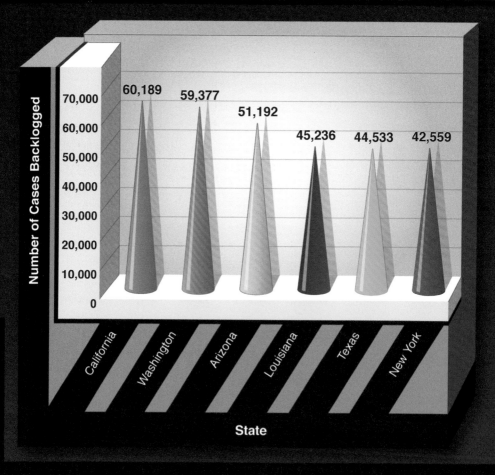

Source: U.S. Department of Justice, *Audit of the Convicted Offender DNA Backlog Reduction Program*, March 2009. ww.usdoj.gov.

Do Law Enforcement DNA Databases Threaten Civil Liberties?

> **While some have raised concerns about the privacy ... rights of persons accused of serious crimes, DNA testing of arrestees can actually protect civil liberties.**
>
> —DNA Saves, an organization that works to educate policy makers and the public about the value of forensic DNA in solving crime.

> **DNA testing, like any powerful tool—and particularly any powerful tool in the hands of the government— must be used carefully. If abused, it can infringe on the privacy and civil liberties of Americans while doing little to prevent crime.**
>
> —Patrick Leahy, a U.S. senator from Vermont and chair of the Senate Judiciary Committee.

The Fourth Amendment to the U.S. Constitution guarantees the right to protection from unreasonable search or seizure. It also states that searches or seizures of people, places, or things are not to be done without probable cause. Of course, when the Constitution was written more than 200 years ago, no one was even aware of DNA, let alone that it could be used to connect crimes with criminals. When the founding fathers spoke of searches and seizures, they were specifically referring to physical acts, such as searching someone's home and taking away property. But today many people argue that large databases, especially those that include DNA profiles of suspects who have been arrested or detained for a crime but not yet convicted, violate the Fourth Amendment.

Others disagree with that perspective. Their belief is that the expansion of DNA databases means more criminals will be caught and convicted, and thereby prevented from committing more crimes. They also maintain that collecting DNA from people who are arrested is not a violation of civil liberties. Criminal defense attorney Nathaniel Burney shares his perspective: "Obviously, this raises eyebrows in certain circles. Taking DNA from people who haven't even been convicted yet? Taking DNA from people who aren't suspected of committing crimes where DNA would even be relevant? Doesn't this violate basic principles of our jurisprudence? Well . . . and this is a defense attorney talking here . . . no."[44]

> " Today many people argue that large databases, especially those that include DNA profiles of suspects who have been arrested or detained for a crime but not yet convicted, violate the Fourth Amendment. "

The Evolution of CODIS

When the FBI's CODIS database became fully operational in 1998, its DNA profiles were limited to convicted criminals who had committed the most violent homicides and sexual crimes. The reasoning at the time was that the database's focus should be on the DNA of those who were most likely to commit repeat crimes and who were also likely to leave biological evidence at the crime scene. Over time the database was expanded to include DNA profiles of everyone who was convicted of a violent crime, and later all those who were convicted of a felony, such as armed robbery or arson. Then the FBI moved beyond convictions to expand CODIS even further. Legislation known as the DNA Fingerprint Act of 2005 vastly expanded the FBI's authority to collect and retain DNA samples.

As of 2009, CODIS includes DNA profiles of all individuals who have been arrested for a federal crime by any U.S. law enforcement agency, as well as those who have been convicted. The database also includes DNA profiles of noncitizens who are being detained by the federal government. Thomas Bologna, president of the DNA testing group Orchid Cellmark, explains why he supports this action by the FBI:

> Our support reflects our experience as a major DNA testing provider both here and in the U.K., where the DNA

database includes most arrestees and approximately half of crime scene evidence samples successfully match a profile already in the DNA database, contributing significantly to crime fighting efforts. We believe further expansion of forensic DNA testing through these regulations will enable U.S. law enforcement officials to solve crimes more rapidly and will also help prevent the repeat offenses committed by some criminals before they are convicted.[45]

Those who do not share Bologna's views say that hundreds of thousands of potentially innocent people will have their DNA on file with the FBI. According to Matthew Strugar, an attorney with the Center for Constitutional Rights, this represents an "unjustified and unnecessary expansion of the federal DNA database." He points to the original purpose of the database and says that it has now expanded far beyond that. "An arrest is not a determination of wrongdoing," Strugar writes. "Instead, our foundational constitutional principles mandate a complex series of checks to protect the innocent from accusation without requisite proof. These include a prompt hearing to ensure probable cause existed for an arrest . . . and a presumption of innocence until proven guilty."[46] Struger believes the expansion of CODIS conflicts with those principles.

> As of 2009, CODIS includes DNA profiles of all individuals who have been arrested for a federal crime by any U.S. law enforcement agency, as well as noncitizens being detained by the federal government.

State DNA Database Laws

Currently, all 50 states require that DNA samples be taken from all convicted sex offenders. In addition, all but Idaho, Nebraska, and New Hampshire require that anyone who is convicted of a felony provide a DNA sample for the state's database. Legislators in New Hampshire were considering such legislation in 2008, but they voted it down. State attorney general Kelly Ayotte was angry when the bill was defeated. "It is wrong," she writes, "to value the rights of convicted felons and sex offenders over public safety. Yet that is what a majority of our state representatives did recently when they voted down legislation . . . allowing the State Police Forensic Laboratory to obtain DNA samples from convicted felons and all sexual offenders for inclusion in the FBI's Combined DNA Index System (CODIS)."[47]

> As of August 2009, 17 states had laws in place requiring the collection of DNA from people arrested for various crimes, and a number of others had legislation pending.

Ayotte refers to an elderly woman from Indiana who was brutally raped in 2000 and another elderly woman who was raped and murdered the following year. Law enforcement officials later learned that the perpetrator in both instances had been convicted of property crimes in 1998. Ayotte says this should never have been allowed to happen: "Had the state obtained a DNA sample after the 1998 felony conviction, the rape and murder of the elderly woman in 2001 would have been prevented."[48]

Such a crime might have been prevented in the states that have followed the FBI's lead and expanded their databases to include arrestees as well as convicted felons. As of August 2009, 17 states had laws in place requiring the collection of DNA from people arrested for various crimes, and a number of others had legislation pending. One state that expanded its DNA database to include arrestees was Florida. On June 16, 2009, the governor signed into law a bill that mandates collecting DNA from offenders arrested for and/or charged with any felony. Gerald Bailey, commissioner of the Florida Department of Law Enforcement, strongly supports this legislation, as he explains: "Some have suggested the DNA Database should only store samples from those convicted of crimes. We disagree. Only about half of arrests result in successful prosecution. Often cases are dropped for reasons that have nothing to do with the guilt or innocence of the defendant." Bailey says that adding the DNA of people who are arrested for felonies will result in vastly improved crime-fighting abilities on the part of law enforcement. "Adding felony arrestees will result in more crimes being solved, repeat offenders taken off the street sooner and lives literally being saved. . . . Florida has successfully put in place the foundation for very powerful public safety policy. No other tool has the ability to prevent violent crimes as efficiently and effectively. Our citizens expect this. We think they deserve it."[49]

Oklahoma is another state that has expanded its DNA database. On May 20, 2009, legislation took effect that makes it a requirement for DNA samples to be taken from all illegal immigrants who are arrested. The law also expands the database beyond just felony convictions and requires people convicted of numerous misdemeanors to provide DNA. The reasoning behind this part of the legislation is that many criminals use plea deals to reduce their conviction to a misdemeanor rather than a felony. Since the law took effect, those in Oklahoma who are convicted of assault and battery, domestic abuse, stalking, resisting arrest, or pointing a firearm are required to provide a DNA sample. The same is true for negligent homicide, destruction of property, breaking and entering a dwelling place, or causing a personal injury accident while driving under the influence.

> " Since the law took effect, those in Oklahoma who are convicted of assault and battery, domestic abuse, stalking, resisting arrest, or pointing a firearm are required to provide a DNA sample. "

This expansion has stirred controversy in the state, with many saying it infringes on individual privacy rights. Bob Ravitz, Oklahoma County chief public defender, is one who is disturbed by the new law. "The issue is how far do you want to go?" he asks. "If you took away everyone's constitutional rights you'd solve more crimes, for sure. The question is where does it stop?"[50]

Sensitive Information on File

Some people who argue on behalf of expanding DNA databases to include arrestees argue that collecting DNA is much the same as collecting and data banking fingerprints. As Burney explains:

> For more than 45 years, it's been well-settled that someone who's been arrested has a diminished expectation of privacy in his own identity. He can be compelled to give fingerprints, have his mug shot taken, and give ID information. DNA is no different than fingerprints—a unique identifier that helps law enforcement find the right suspect, and eliminate the wrong suspect. In fact, DNA is more precise than photos or fingerprints, so the government interest in obtaining it is even stronger.[51]

The difference, however, is that fingerprints do not reveal genetic information about a suspect. They are merely images of the raised portion of the fingertips and are examined visually to compare with other prints in an attempt to identify a suspect. But according to an August 2007 report published by the American Constitution Society for Law and Policy, DNA has very different implications. The authors of the report write:

> By contrast, DNA, which must be extracted from a tissue sample and mined for data, contains exactly the kind of information that raises privacy and other civil liberties concerns. Research conducted to expand our knowledge of what can be revealed by examining a person's DNA continues; as of this writing, samples of DNA can provide insights into familial connections, physical attributes, genetic mutations, ancestry and disease predisposition.[52]

The authors add that as science continues to advance, the genetic information that is available in DNA will undoubtedly grow. "Genetic information could be used in discriminatory ways and may include information that the person whose DNA it is does not wish to [be known]. Repeated claims that human behaviors such as aggression, substance addiction, criminal tendency, and sexual orientation can be explained by genetics render law enforcement's collection, use and retention of DNA potentially prone to abuse."[53]

Familial DNA

Those who caution that expansive DNA databases are eroding constitutional rights often use the term "CODIS creep." This refers to an attempt by the government to take DNA samples collected for one purpose and use them for an entirely different purpose. For example, when a DNA database yields only a partial match with a suspect, it is likely that he or she did not commit the crime. But if the DNA is a close partial match, that could mean the real criminal is the father, mother, son, daughter, or sibling of the person who was tested. When such a match is made, law enforcement officials have a probable cause to find and test the new suspect. This is known as a familial DNA test, and some criminal law studies have shown that if databases were used to search for family members, they could yield an estimated 40 percent more matches.

> " Those who caution that expansive DNA databases are eroding constitutional rights often use the term 'CODIS creep.' "

Yet even though more criminals could be caught with familial DNA, it is a controversial issue. Barry C. Scheck of the Innocence Project says that he would support such searches if they were authorized and carefully regulated by Congress. But, he states, "I don't think there can be any doubt that when the U.S. Congress passed the DNA Identification Act of 1994, it did not think for a nanosecond that it was authorizing a database that was going to be used for purposes of familial searches."[54]

Not everyone agrees with Scheck's viewpoint, however. People who believe that familial DNA searches should be allowed say that it increases law enforcement's ability to track down and arrest criminals through their family members. Without the ability to do that, they claim, many violent criminals would remain free to commit even more crimes. One enthusiastic proponent of the practice is Frederick Bieber of Harvard University's Brigham and Women's Hospital. "Does crime cluster in families?" he asks. "We know that it does." He adds that nearly half of the inmates in federal and state prisons have a family member who has also been incarcerated. "If crime didn't occur in clusters of families, all this would be an academic conversation."[55]

An Ongoing Controversy

When considering the various factors involved with DNA testing, DNA databases are among the most controversial. Some people are convinced that databases should be expanded to include DNA profiles of everyone who is arrested for a crime, while others argue that this is a violation of civil liberties. Whether these two sides will ever reach an agreement on the issue is doubtful, since all who have an opinion are equally passionate about what they believe.

Primary Source Quotes*

Do Law Enforcement DNA Databases Threaten Civil Liberties?

66 Including felony arrests means more samples in the DNA database and more crimes solved. It also means crimes will be solved faster and, most important, crimes will be prevented. 99

—Gerald Bailey, "DNA Can Prevent Crime," *Miami Herald*, June 29, 2009. www.miamiherald.com.

Bailey is the commissioner of the Florida Department of Law Enforcement.

66 When the person's DNA profile is entered into the database and it matches the profile of a perpetrator of a serious crime, we've caught a potentially dangerous person. But in my view the logistics and the potential misuse of DNA evidence raise too many questions to go forward with arrestee databases. 99

—Matt Kelley, "The Debate over DNA Databases," Criminal Justice—Change.org, July 20, 2009. http://criminaljustice.change.org

Kelley is the online communications manager for the Innocence Project.

Bracketed quotes indicate conflicting positions.

* Editor's Note: While the definition of a primary source can be narrowly or broadly defined, for the purposes of Compact Research, a primary source consists of: 1) results of original research presented by an organization or researcher; 2) eyewitness accounts of events, personal experience, or work experience; 3) first-person editorials offering pundits' opinions; 4) government officials presenting political plans and/or policies; 5) representatives of organizations presenting testimony or policy.

Primary Source Quotes

66 What business does the government have collecting our DNA—locally and nationally? Just on the off chance that sometime, somewhere in the country, the DNA might identify someone who was previously convicted or who didn't show up for court? What are the odds of that? Why do they think this should trump our personal privacy and bodily integrity? 99

—James C. Harrington, "They Want a Piece of You: DNA Database Proposal Is Invasive and Unconstitutional," *Newspaper Tree*, February 10, 2009. www.newspapertree.com.

Harrington is the director of the Texas Civil Rights Project, a nonprofit foundation that promotes civil rights and justice throughout the state.

66 Like fingerprints, DNA is [a] powerful identification and crime solving tool. The public's interest in safety far outweighs any interest a convicted felon or sex offender has in the identification characteristics of their DNA. 99

—Kelly Ayotte, "On DNA Testing, NH Favors Felons over Public Safety," Manchester *Union Leader*, June 12, 2008. www.unionleader.com.

Ayotte is the former attorney general of New Hampshire.

66 Law enforcement's use of these tools to search, profile and store the DNA of those who have not been convicted of a crime, without a court order or individualized suspicion, has already exceeded reasonable constitutional protections. 99

—Tania Simoncelli and Sheldon Krimsky, "A New Era of DNA Collections: At What Cost to Civil Liberties?" American Constitution Society for Law and Policy, August 2007. www.bioforensics.com.

Simoncelli is a science advisor for the American Civil Liberties Union, and Krimsky is a professor of urban and environmental policy and planning at Tufts University's School of Arts and Sciences.

66 For minority populations who are already dispropor- tionately in the [DNA] database, you're approaching a scenario where nearly a majority of some populations— minority based populations—are going to find them- selves under genetic surveillance by the government. 99

—Stephen Mercer, interviewed by Lucky Severson, "Familial DNA Testing," *Religion & Ethics*, PBS, March 6, 2009. www.pbs.org.

Mercer is an attorney from Maryland who specializes in DNA issues.

66 DNA profiles are different from fingerprints, which are useful only for identification. DNA can provide in- sights into many intimate aspects of people and their families including susceptibility to particular diseas- es, legitimacy of birth, and perhaps predispositions to certain behaviors and sexual orientation. 99

—U.S. Human Genome Project, "DNA Forensics," June 16, 2009. www.ornl.gov.

The Human Genome Project was formed to identify all the genes in human DNA, develop an expansive understanding of them, and store the information in databases.

66 Neither the United States nor the United Kingdom have any models for the kind of comprehensive pri- vacy regulations that would prevent the government from sharing DNA profiles in law enforcement data- bases with insurance companies, employers, schools, and the private sector. 99

—Jeffrey Rosen, "Genetic Surveillance for All," *Slate*, March 17, 2009. www.slate.com.

Rosen is a law professor at George Washington University and the legal affairs editor of the *New Republic*.

Do Law Enforcement DNA Databases Threaten Civil Liberties?

- As of May 2009 the FBI's CODIS database contained more than **7 million offender DNA profiles** and **272,000 forensic profiles** (created from crime scene evidence) and was the largest forensic database in the world.

- In 2007 more than **90 DNA database expansion bills** were introduced in 36 states.

- In January 2007 New Mexico became the first state to require DNA samples to be taken for most **felony arrests**, in addition to convictions.

- In 2008 the FBI's CODIS database produced nearly **81,000 DNA matches** with offender profiles and more than **14,000 matches** with forensic profiles.

- As of July 2009, 21 states allowed DNA samples to be taken from all those who have been **detained or arrested for a felony offense**.

- In 2006 the Minnesota Court of Appeals struck down a state law authorizing the **collection of DNA from arrestees**, saying that the practice violated the constitutional requirement that searches may not be conducted without a warrant.

- In April 2009 the FBI announced that it had expanded its CODIS database to include DNA of everyone who is **detained or arrested for federal crimes**, as well as non-U.S. citizens who are being detained in the United States.

States with Arrestees in DNA Databases

All but three U.S. states have legislation in place that requires DNA samples to be taken from convicted felons and filed in a database. As of June 2009, 17 states had expanded their laws to include DNA from people who have been arrested for certain crimes. This is a source of controversy because those who oppose such practices say it is a violation of privacy to keep DNA profiles on file of people who have not been proven guilty of any crime.

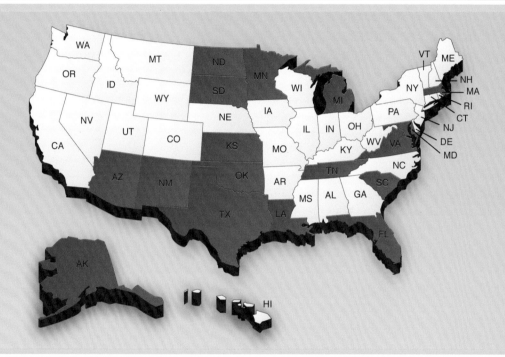

 States that have added DNA of arrestees to DNA database

Sources: National Conference of State Legislatures, "State Laws on DNA Data Banks Qualifying Offenses, Others Who Must Provide Sample," February 2009. www.ncsl.org; ProPublica, "Where States Stand on DNA Collection," May 5, 2009. www.propublica.org.

- The expansion of CODIS is expected to accelerate the growth rate of the database from **80,000 new entries a year** to an estimated **1.2 million per year** by 2012.

- According to Stanford University Law School professor Hank Greely, African Americans make up **40 percent** of DNA profiles in CODIS, although they represent just **12 percent** of the U.S. population.

- In 2008 California's attorney general began to allow **familial DNA searching** in the state's DNA database, which is the largest state database in the country.

- Twelve states do not have laws requiring the destruction of DNA samples after a conviction has been overturned by the courts, which means the **DNA of potentially innocent people remains on file.**

Genetic Profiles

Collecting DNA profiles from people who have been arrested but not convicted of a crime raises certain civil liberties concerns, namely that highly personal genetic information (such as ancestry, intelligence,and likelihood of developing certain illnesses) will be available to law enforcement authorities. This loss of privacy is generally accepted where convicted offenders are concerned, but it is controversial when it involves a person who has not been convicted of any crime. This table shows the types of genetic information that may appear in DNA databases.

Genetic information potentially on file when DNA samples are in databases
Eye color
Hair color
Race
Skin tone
Facial structure and features, such as the width of the nose, spacing of the eyes, or height of the lips
Right- or left-handedness
Ancestry/Familial connections
Genetic mutations that could lead to diseases or disorders
Musical, artistic, or athletic aptitude
Intelligence quotient (IQ)

Sources: Gautam Naik, "To Sketch a Thief: Genes Draw Likeness of Suspects," *Wall Street Journal*, March 27, 2009. http://online.wsj.com; Tania Simoncelli and Sheldon Krimsky, *A New Era of DNA Collections: At What Cost to Civil Liberties?* American Constitution Society for Law and Policy, August 2007; Matthew Struger, "Comments of the Center for Constitutional Rights on Department of Justice, Proposed Rules: 'DNA-Sample Collection Under the DNA Fingerprint Act of 2005 and the Adam Walsh Child Protection and Safety Act of 2006,' 28 C.F.R. Part 28 (April 18, 2008)." May 19, 2008. http://ccrjustice.org.

Racial Bias

In addition to convicted offenders, the FBI CODIS database now contains DNA profiles of anyone who is arrested for a federal crime. Many see this as a violation of civil liberties because the DNA of potentially innocent people remains on file. Of special concern is the disproportionate number of Hispanics and African Americans who are arrested and sentenced in federal courts, as this chart shows. The result, some experts say, is a racially biased database. They contend that being in the DNA database increases the risk of being falsely accused and even convicted of serious crimes.

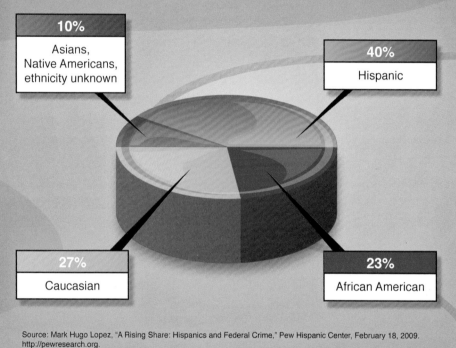

10% Asians, Native Americans, ethnicity unknown

40% Hispanic

27% Caucasian

23% African American

Source: Mark Hugo Lopez, "A Rising Share: Hispanics and Federal Crime," Pew Hispanic Center, February 18, 2009. http://pewresearch.org.

- In December 2008 the European Court of Human Rights ruled that Britain violated international law by collecting **DNA profiles from innocent people**, including **children as young as 10**.

Key People and Advocacy Groups

American Civil Liberties Union (ACLU): The ACLU, which refers to itself as the "nation's guardian of liberty," is an organization that opposes the expansion of DNA databases to include profiles of people who have been arrested or detained for crimes.

Kirk Bloodsworth: The first death row prisoner to be exonerated and pardoned after DNA testing showed that he had not committed the crime for which he had been convicted.

Center for Constitutional Rights: An organization that is dedicated to advancing and protecting the rights guaranteed by the U.S. Constitution, and which has expressed its strong opposition to expanding DNA databases to include profiles of people arrested or detained for crimes.

Francis Crick: A British scientist who in 1953 discovered the genetic code, which enabled scientists to predict characteristics by studying DNA.

DNA Initiative: A federal agency that works for increased funding, training, and assistance to forensic scientists and law enforcement professionals so that DNA technology reaches its full potential to solve crimes, protect the innocent, and identify missing persons.

Innocence Project: A national litigation and public policy organization dedicated to exonerating wrongfully convicted people through DNA testing.

Alec Jeffreys: An English geneticist who discovered that certain regions of DNA contain sequences that are repeated over and over again and that the number of repeated sections differs from individual to individual. This finding allowed him to develop a technique to perform human identity tests using DNA samples.

Mitch Morrissey: A district attorney from Denver who is an outspoken advocate for expanding DNA testing.

National Human Genome Research Institute: A federal agency that supports the development of resources and technology that will accelerate genome research and its application to human health.

Colin Pitchfork: A man from Bristol, England, who raped and murdered two teenage girls and was the first person ever to be indicted and convicted based on DNA evidence.

Barry C. Scheck and Peter J. Neufeld: Attorneys at the Benjamin N. Cardozo School of Law at Yeshiva University who founded the Innocence Project advocacy group in 1992.

Jayann and David Sepich: After the 2003 murder of their 22-year-old daughter, Katie, the Sepichs founded DNA Saves. The organization works toward the passage of laws nationwide to require collection of DNA for felony arrests for inclusion in state and federal crime databases.

William S. Sessions: The former director of the FBI who is outspoken in his belief that all prisoners who request postconviction DNA testing should be able to have it.

Chronology

1988
Colorado becomes the first state to require criminals who have committed sex crimes to provide a DNA sample to law enforcement officials.

1953
Based largely on X-ray photographs of DNA by chemist Rosalind Franklin, scientists James Watson and Francis Crick publish their discovery of DNA's winding, two-stranded chemical structure and coin it the "double helix."

1985
English geneticist Alec Jeffreys discovers that certain regions of DNA contain sequences that are repeated over and over again and that the number of repeated sections differs from person to person, meaning that each individual has unique DNA. This leads Jeffreys to develop the first DNA profiling test, and he coins the term "DNA fingerprint."

1950   1960   1970   1980   1990

1962
Scientists James Watson and Francis Crick are awarded the Nobel Prize for their work on DNA.

1987
Colin Pitchfork, a man from Bristol, England, who raped and murdered two teenage girls, becomes the first person ever to be indicted and convicted using DNA evidence.

1989
Gary Dotson and David Vasquez become the first two prisoners in the United States to be exonerated by DNA evidence.

1990
The Federal Bureau of Investigation begins a pilot project called the Combined DNA Index System, or CODIS, a national database of DNA profiles.

1992
The Innocence Project is founded in 1992 by Barry C. Scheck and Peter J. Neufeld at the Benjamin N. Cardozo School of Law at Yeshiva University to assist convicted offenders who could possibly be exonerated through DNA testing.

1993
After spending more than eight years in prison for a sexual assault and murder that he did not commit, Kirk Bloodsworth becomes the first death row prisoner to be exonerated by postconviction DNA testing.

1995
The world's first DNA database is launched in the United Kingdom.

1998
The FBI's national DNA database, CODIS, becomes fully operational.

2004
President George W. Bush signs into law the Justice for All Act of 2004, which launches the National Institute of Justice's DNA Initiative.

2007
A comprehensive study commissioned by the U.S. Department of Justice shows that it is prudent to expand DNA evidence collection beyond homicides and sexual assaults to property crimes.

1995   1998   2001   2004   2007

1994
The U.S. Congress passes the DNA Identification Act of 1994, which authorizes the collection of violent offenders' DNA in a national database.

2006
The DNA Fingerprint Act of 2005 is signed into law in 2006 by President George W. Bush.

2008
The U.S. Supreme Court agrees to hear the case of William Osborne, a convicted felon who was denied postconviction DNA testing by the state of Alaska. The following year the Court rules that DNA testing is not a constitutional right and the power to determine if such testing is warranted should be left up to the states.

2009
The FBI announces that it has expanded its CODIS database to include not only DNA samples from convicted criminals but also those who have been arrested or detained for federal crimes, as well as non-U.S. citizens who are being detained in the United States.

The National Research Council releases a report that reveals serious flaws in forensic crime laboratories throughout the United States.

Related Organizations

American Civil Liberties Union (ACLU)
125 Broad St., 18th Floor
New York, NY 10004
phone: (212) 549-2500
fax: (212) 549-2646
e-mail: aclu@aclu.org • Web site: www.aclu.org

The ACLU, which refers to itself as the "nation's guardian of liberty," works with courts, legislatures, and communities to ensure that everyone in the United States is afforded the rights and liberties guaranteed by the Constitution. Its Web site's search engine produces numerous articles about DNA testing, databases, and other issues.

Center for Constitutional Rights
666 Broadway, 7th Floor
New York, NY 10012
phone: (212) 614-6464
Web site: http://ccrjustice.org

The Center for Constitutional Rights is a legal and educational organization that is dedicated to advancing and protecting the rights that are guaranteed by the U.S. Constitution and the Universal Declaration of Human Rights. Its Web site features current and past legal cases, news releases, fact sheets, reports and publications, and links to videoclips and podcasts.

DNA Initiative
National Institute of Justice
810 Seventh St. NW
Washington, DC 20531
phone: (202) 307-2942
fax: (202) 307-9907
Web site: www.dna.gov

The DNA Initiative works for increased funding, training, and assistance to forensic scientists and law enforcement professionals so that DNA technology reaches its full potential to solve crimes, protect the innocent, and identify missing persons. Its Web site has a wealth of information about forensic DNA, including the basics of DNA typing, statistics, DNA databases, and research and development.

DNA Saves

phone: (575) 361-1931
e-mail: jsepich@dnasaves.org • Web site: www.dnasaves.org

Founded by Jayann and David Sepich, whose daughter was murdered, DNA Saves is committed to working with every state to pass laws allowing DNA to be taken upon arrest and to provide meaningful funding for DNA programs. Its Web site offers information about state DNA legislation, a collection of facts, studies, privacy rights, and stories about people who have been murdered and their killers caught because of DNA evidence.

Federal Bureau of Investigation (FBI)

J. Edgar Hoover Building
935 Pennsylvania Ave. NW
Washington, DC 20535-0001
phone: (202) 324-3000
Web site: www.fbi.gov

The FBI's mission is to protect and defend the United States against terrorist and foreign intelligence threats, and to enforce the country's criminal laws. Its Web site features a number of articles related to DNA evidence as well as news releases, congressional testimonies, facts and figures, and an FBI Youth section that details how FBI agents investigate crimes.

Human Genome Project

U.S. Department of Energy Office of Science
1000 Independence Ave. SW
Washington, DC 20585
phone: (202) 586-5430; toll-free: (800) 342-5363
fax: (202) 586-4403
Web site: http://genomics.energy.gov

The Human Genome Project is a genetic research agency of the U.S. Department of Energy's Office of Science. Its Web site features a good variety of information about DNA evidence, including what DNA is, how DNA forensics works and the technologies that are used, ethical and legal issues, and links to many other articles.

Innocence Project
100 Fifth Ave., 3rd Floor
New York, NY 10011
phone: (212) 364-5340
e-mail: info@innocenceproject.org • Web site: www.innocenceproject.org

The Innocence Project is dedicated to exonerating wrongfully convicted people through DNA testing and reforming the criminal justice system to prevent future injustice. Its Web site features a number of publications related to DNA evidence, such as news releases, fact sheets, and stories about people who were convicted of violent crimes and later exonerated because of DNA evidence.

The Justice Project
1025 Vermont Ave. NW, 3rd Floor
Washington, DC 20005
phone: (202) 638-5855
e-mail: info@thejusticeproject.org • Web site: www.thejusticeproject.org

The Justice Project works to fight injustice and increase fairness and accuracy in the criminal justice system. Its Web site features testimonies, reports and studies, news releases, and stories about people who have been wrongfully accused, convicted, and imprisoned.

National Human Genome Research Institute (NHGRI)
Building 31, Room 4B09
31 Center Dr., MSC 2152
9000 Rockville Pike
Bethesda, MD 20892-2152
phone: (301) 402-0911
fax: (301) 402-2218
Web site: www.genome.gov

The NHGRI, which is part of the National Institutes of Health, supports the development of resources and technology that will accelerate genome research and its application to human health. Its Web site offers educational fact sheets about DNA, articles, and a link to a section titled "DNA from the Beginning," which is an animated primer on the basics of DNA, genes, and heredity.

National Institutes of Health Office of Science Education (OSE)

Office of Science Policy, OD, NIH

Building 1, Room 103

9000 Rockville Pike

Bethesda, MD 20892

phone: (301) 496-2122

fax: (301) 402-1759

Web site: http://science.education.nih.gov

The OSE coordinates science education activities at the National Institutes of Health, as well as developing and sponsoring science education projects in house. These programs serve elementary, secondary, and college students; teachers; and the public. Its Web site's search engine produces numerous publications related to DNA, including educational booklets, articles, fact sheets, and the *Findings* online magazine.

U.S. Bureau of Justice Statistics

810 Seventh St. NW

Washington, DC 20531

phone: (202) 307-0765

e-mail: askbjs@usdoj.gov • Web site: www.ojp.gov/bjs

The Bureau of Justice Statistics is the United States' primary source for criminal justice statistics. Its Web site links to numerous publications and news releases related to crime, the justice system, courts and sentencing, homicide trends, and the FBI's yearly Uniform Crime Reports.

U.S. Department of Justice

950 Pennsylvania Ave. NW

Washington, DC 20530-0001

phone: (202) 514-2000

e-mail: askdoj@usdoj.gov • Web site: www.usdoj.gov

The mission of the Department of Justice is to enforce U.S. law, ensure public safety against foreign and domestic threats, provide federal leadership in preventing and controlling crime, seek just punishment for those guilty of unlawful behavior, and ensure fair and impartial administration of justice for all Americans. Its Web site offers a wide variety of publications that cover issues such as DNA testing, databases, and the various types of crime that DNA is used to solve.

For Further Research

Books

Jay D. Aronson, *Genetic Witness: Science, Law, and Controversy in the Making of DNA Profiling.* New Brunswick, NJ: Rutgers University Press, 2007.

D.B. Beres and Anna Prokos, *Crime Scene: True-Life Forensic Files: Dusting and DNA.* New York: Scholastic, 2008.

George "Woody" Clarke, *Justice and Science: Trials and Triumphs of DNA Evidence.* New Brunswick, NJ: Rutgers University Press, 2008.

Sue Hamilton, *DNA Analysis: Forensic Fluids & Follicles.* Edina, MN: Abdo, 2008.

Brian Innes, *DNA and Body Evidence.* Armonk, NY: Sharp Focus, 2008.

David E. Newton, *DNA Evidence and Forensic Science.* New York: Facts On File, 2008.

Michael Newton, *Encyclopedia of Crime Scene Investigation.* New York: Facts On File, 2008.

Mark Schultz, Zander Cannon, and Kevin Cannon, *The Stuff of Life: A Graphic Guide to Genetics and DNA.* New York: Hill and Wang, 2009.

Periodicals

Tresa Baldas, "Crime Lab Scandal Adds Detroit to Nationwide Group," *Legal Intelligencer*, October 17, 2008.

Joan Biskupic, "Court: Prisoners Don't Have Right to Evidence," *USA Today*, June 19, 2009.

Economist, "Throw It Out: DNA and Human Rights," December 6, 2008.

Becky Gillette, "Better Funding Urged for DNA Testing," *Mississippi Business Journal*, January 19, 2009.

Victor Goode, "If They'd Been Black . . . Would Justice Have Been Served for the Duke Lacrosse Players If They Were Not White and Well-Off?" *Colorlines*, November/December 2007.

Julie Johnson, "More DNA Evidence Going Under Microscope," *Sacramento (CA) Bee*, July 19, 2009.

Barbara L. Jones, "Minnesota Supreme Court: DNA Collection Challenged as an Unreasonable Search," *Minnesota Lawyer*, April 7, 2008.

Matthew G. Kaiser, "Case May Be About Lab Reports, but Will Seal the Future of DNA," *Recorder*, July 18, 2008.

Roger Koppl, "What's Wrong with CSI," *Forbes*, June 2, 2008.

Steven Kreytak, "Dispute over Yogurt Case DNA," *Austin (TX) American Statesman*, June 19, 2009.

Joan Lee, "A Small Comfort for Sex Assault Victims (DNA Evidence on Sex Crimes)," *Connecticut Law Tribune*, September 3, 2007.

Mike McKee, "High Court Appears OK with Cold-Hit Science (Use of DNA Evidence)," *Recorder*, May 9, 2008.

Christian Nolan, "Recent Cases Stir Up DNA Debate," *Connecticut Law Tribune*, January 12, 2009.

Gina Sikes, "Young and Murdered: How Their Killers Were Finally Caught," *Cosmopolitan*, February 2008.

Alex Tresniowski, "She Sent the Wrong Man to Prison," *People Weekly*, March 16, 2009.

Internet Sources

Peter Dizikes, "Your DNA Is a Snitch," *Salon*, February 17, 2009. www.salon.com/env/feature/2009/02/17/genetic_testing.

Human Genome Project, "DNA Forensics," June 19, 2009. www.ornl.gov/sci/techresources/Human_Genome/elsi/forensics.shtml#6.

Ellen Nakashima, "From DNA of Family, a Tool to Make Arrests," *Washington Post*, April 21, 2008. www.washingtonpost.com/wp-dyn/content/article/2008/04/20/AR2008042002388.html.

National Research Council of the National Academies, *Strengthening Forensic Science in the United States: A Path Forward*. Washington: National Academies Press, 2009. http://books.nap.edu/openbook.php?record_id=12589&page=R1

New York Times, "DNA Evidence," June 18, 2009. http://topics.nytimes.com/top/reference/timestopics/subjects/d/dna_evidence/index.html.

John K. Roman et al., *The DNA Field Experiment: Cost-Effectiveness Analysis of the Use of DNA in the Investigation of High-Volume Crimes*, Urban Institute, March 2008. www.ncjrs.gov/pdffiles1/nij/grants/222318.pdf.

Source Notes

Overview

1. Quoted in Federal Bureau of Investigation, Baltimore, "Washington, D.C. Man Convicted in the Murder of Dunbar Armored Car Employee in Prince George's County," press release, June 3, 2009. http://baltimore.fbi.gov.
2. National Human Genome Research Institute, "Deoxyribonucleic Acid (DNA)," June 24, 2009. www.genome.gov.
3. John K. Roman, Shannon Reid, Jay Reid, Aaron Chalfin, William Adams, and Carly Knight, *The DNA Field Experiment: Cost-Effectiveness Analysis of the Use of DNA in the Investigation of High-Volume Crimes*, Urban Institute, April 2008. www.ncjrs.gov.
4. Nicholas D. Kristof, "Is Rape Serious?" *New York Times*, April 29, 2009. www.nytimes.com.
5. Human Genome Project, "DNA Forensics," June 16, 2009. www.ornl.gov.
6. Federal Bureau of Investigation, "Science and Technology in the Name of Justice, Part 2: FBI DNA Database Passes an Important Milestone," February 3, 2004. www.fbi.gov.
7. U.S. Department of Justice, "Using DNA to Solve Property Crimes," June 16, 2008. www.ojp.usdoj.gov.
8. Quoted in WISN News, "Wrongly Convicted Man Released from Prison," January 9, 2009. www.wisn.com.
9. Supreme Court of the United States, *District Attorney's Office for the Third Judicial District et al. v. Osborne,* June 18, 2009. www.supremecourtus.gov.
10. Shaila Dewan, "Prosecutors Block Access to DNA Testing for Inmates," *New York Times*, May 18, 2009. www.nytimes.com.
11. Gerald Bailey, "DNA Can Prevent Crime," *Miami Herald*, June 29, 2009. www.miamiherald.com.
12. Patrick Leahy, "Statement of Senator Patrick Leahy (D-Vt.), Chairman, Senate Judiciary Committee, on Expanded DNA Collection by the Federal Government," United States Senator Patrick Leahy, April 24, 2008. http://leahy.senate.gov.
13. Quoted in Ellen Nakashima, "From DNA of Family, a Tool to Make Arrests," *Washington Post*, April 21, 2008. www.washingtonpost.com.

How Conclusive Is DNA Evidence in Solving Crimes?

14. Steven D. Levitt, "Are the F.B.I.'s Probabilities About DNA Matches Crazy?" *New York Times* Freakonomics blog, August 19, 2008. http://freakonomics.blogs.nytimes.com.
15. Robert Rowe, "8 Things an Arsonist Should Know," Pyrocop, 2008. www.pyrocop.com.
16. Quoted in Allison Bourg, "Maryland Police Use DNA to Make Arson Case," MassCops, January 27, 2009. www.masscops.com.
17. Quoted in Tresa Baldas, "Crime Lab Scandal Adds Detroit to Nationwide Group," *Legal Intelligencer*, October 17, 2008.
18. Quoted in Baldas, "Crime Lab Scandal Adds Detroit to Nationwide Group."
19. Quoted in Death Penalty Information Center, "Accuracy of DNA 'Matches' to Definitely Identify Suspects Questioned," 2008. www.deathpenaltyinfo.org.
20. George "Woody" Clarke, *Justice and Science: Trials and Triumphs of DNA Evidence.* New Brunswick, NJ: Rutgers University Press, 2008, p. 2.

How Effective Is DNA Testing for Correcting Justice System Errors?

21. Sean Sweeney, "Fort Lauderdale-Miami Criminal Law Appeals: Flawed Eye Witness Testimony & Photo Line Ups," South Florida Criminal Attorney Blog, January 18, 2009. www.southfloridacriminalattorneyblog.com.

22. Quoted in Adam Liptak, "Study of Wrongful Convictions Raises Questions Beyond DNA," *New York Times*, July 23, 2007. http://select.nytimes.com.

23. Brandon L. Garrett, "Judging Innocence," *Columbia Law Review*, January 2008. www.columbialawreview.org.

24. Garrett, "Judging Innocence."

25. Garrett, "Judging Innocence."

26. Radley Balko, "No Money, No Justice," *Reason*, December 2007. www.reason.com.

27. Quoted in Balko, "No Money, No Justice."

28. The Justice Project, *Improving Access to Post-Conviction DNA Testing: A Policy Review*, August 12, 2008. www.thejusticeproject.org.

29. The Justice Project, *Improving Access to Post-Conviction DNA Testing.*

30. Quoted in Democracy Now, "Ryan Matthews Is Free: Death Row Prisoner Convicted as Juvenile Exonerated After 5 Yrs in Jail," August 12, 2004. http://i4.democracynow.org.

31. Quoted in CNN, "Texan Who Died in Prison Cleared of Rape Conviction," February 6, 2009. www.cnn.com.

32. *Seattle Times*, "Expand Use of DNA to Catch Criminals, Exonerate the Innocent," February 4, 2009. http://seattletimes.nwsource.com.

Should Prisoners Have a Right to DNA Testing?

33. FindLaw, "U.S. Constitution: Fourteenth Amendment." http://caselaw.lp.findlaw.com.

34. Samuel A. Alito, *District Attorney's Office for the Third Judicial District et al. v. Osborne,* June 18, 2009. www4.law.cornell.edu.

35. John Paul Stevens, *District Attorney's Office for the Third Judicial District et al. v. Osborne,* June 18, 2009. www.supremecourtus.gov.

36. Robert Morgenthau, "Alaska's Refusal to Use a DNA Test for True Justice Is Shameful," *New York Daily News*, February 27, 2009. www.nydailynews.com.

37. Quoted in Bobby Kerlik, "Pennsylvania Prisoners Seeking Exoneration by DNA May Get Help," *Pittsburgh Tribune-Review*, June 29, 2009. www.pittsburghlive.com.

38. Roman et al., *The DNA Field Experiment.*

39. Quoted in Ben Protess, "The DNA Debacle: How the Federal Government Botched the DNA Backlog Crisis," *ProPublica*, May 5, 2009. www.propublica.org.

40. Kristof, "Is Rape Serious?"

41. John Terzano, "Post-Conviction DNA Testing Shouldn't Depend on Miracles," *Huffington Post*, August 12, 2008. www.huffingtonpost.com.

42. The Justice Project, *Improving Access to Post-Conviction DNA Testing.*

43. The Justice Project, *Improving Access to Post-Conviction DNA Testing.*

Do Law Enforcement DNA Databases Threaten Civil Liberties?

44. Nathaniel Burney, "Mandatory DNA Sampling Constitutional. Expect Ruling to Be Upheld," *Criminal Lawyer*, May 29, 2009. www.burneylawfirm.com.

45. Quoted in Barbara Lindheim, "Orchid Cellmark Applauds Expansion of Federal Forensic DNA Identity Testing to Include All Arrestees," news release, Orchid Cellmark, April 23, 2008. www.orchidcellmark.com.

46. Matthew Strugar, "Comments of the Center for Constitutional Rights on Department of Justice, Proposed Rules: 'DNA-Sample Collection Under the DNA Fingerprint Act of 2005 and the Adam Walsh Child Protection and Safety Act of 2006,' 28 C.F.R. Part 28 (April 18, 2008)," letter to the Office of Legal Policy, May 19, 2008. http://ccrjustice.org.

47. Kelly Ayotte, "On DNA Testing, NH Favors Felons over Public Safety," *Manchester Union Leader*, June 12, 2008. www.unionleader.com.

48. Ayotte, "On DNA Testing, NH Favors Felons over Public Safety."

49. Gerald Bailey, "Pro-Con, Gerald Bailey: Should Florida Take DNA Samples of Suspected Felons Before Conviction? Yes," *TC Palm*, July 13, 2009. www.tcpalm.com.

50. Quoted in Vallery Brown, "DNA Law Stirs Privacy Debate in Oklahoma," *Oklahoman*, June 8, 2009. http://newsok.com.

51. Burney, "Mandatory DNA Sampling Constitutional."

52. Tania Simoncelli and Sheldon Krimsky, "A New Era of DNA Collections: At What Cost to Civil Liberties?" American Constitution Society for Law and Policy, August 2007. www.bioforensics.com.

53. Simoncelli and Krimsky, "A New Era of DNA Collections."

54. Quoted in Jeffrey Rosen, "Genetic Surveillance for All," *Slate*, March 17, 2009. www.slate.com.

55. Quoted in Rosen, "Genetic Surveillance for All."

List of Illustrations

Index

About the Author

Peggy J. Parks holds a bachelor of science degree from Aquinas College in Grand Rapids, Michigan, where she graduated magna cum laude. She has written more than 80 nonfiction educational books for children and young adults, as well as published her own cookbook called *Welcome Home: Recipes, Memories, and Traditions from the Heart*. Parks lives in Muskegon, Michigan, a town that she says inspires her writing because of its location on the shores of Lake Michigan.